maryanne moodie's

MODERN WEAVER

Where
Color
Meets
Loom

ABRAMS,
NEW YORK

CONTENTS

introduction

This book has been nearly two decades in the making. I began my journey as a schoolteacher twenty years ago and then moved on to weaving and teaching weaving. I loved being a teacher, and I learned so much from my students—how to assess a learner and help them on their journey, how to break down skills into manageable steps, and that there are many learning styles and ways to get to the end goal.

I have been a weaver for almost ten years. Most of my education has come from tapestry manuals, fiber art books, and even looking at original modern weavings from the 1970s. I have made many mistakes along the way, but have tried to use them as opportunities to learn more.

This book brings together those twenty years of experience. I have distilled all of my trial and error into a collection of tips and tricks for weavers of all levels.

The collection of projects is divided for beginners, intermediate weavers, and those more advanced in their skills, but was created with the hope that there are projects to interest and challenge weavers of all backgrounds.

In this book, I want to take you from the firm foundations in tools and loom creating to choosing fibers, finding inspiration, and distilling it into a design. This journey can be daunting and exasperating, but I have created a thoughtful process that scaffolds weavers along the way.

Each of my projects is underpinned with a basis in color. I have always had quite a strong relationship with color, and I love experimenting with it. I know that many people do not share this confidence, but in this book you will find all the secrets to creating bold color choices and breaking out of your safe zone.

Most of the materials and tools you need are available to purchase through my website, maryannemoodie.com. I have also included a list of suppliers I know you'll love (page 190).

beginner projects

I teach in-person weaving classes at all levels and also have online courses on my website. The most popular by far are the weavers' basics courses. I love being the gateway for the weaving-curious. The basics are quite simple, and a person who is new to weaving can produce amazing results with a few simple skills. The first few projects in this book are aimed at those of you who are new to weaving: They are here to help you nail down the basics and give you confidence to move forward on your weaving journey.

intermediate projects

Many people are able to grasp the basics of weaving in a few hours. Once you have mastered the skills of tabby, rya, loops, and soumak, I encourage you to move forward and try some trickier projects. Perhaps you're coming to the book with these skills already mastered! In this section, we'll try some out-of-the-box skills, apply them to interesting and new homewares, and even utilize fiber sculpture.

advanced projects

This section is chock-full of projects that tickle my imagination. I have drawn extensively on my years of experience to create these advanced projects and hope you can not only learn some new skills but different ways to apply skills you already know. You will have seen some of these projects among my own work, and I've come up with some never-before-seen projects that I'm excited to share.

color

You could say I've always had a love affair with color. My home and wardrobe are a riotous cacophony of bright hues, jewel tones, and pastels. Some people are drawn to a more simple palette; I am a sucker for a clash—I love surrounding myself with bold combinations.

Growing up, I was told that I had a natural affinity for colors—a knack for knowing how to pair them—and for a long time, I believed it. Then one day, during art class, I was introduced to the color wheel, a simple tool for understanding how colors can be mixed to create new ones. The primary colors—yellow, blue, and red—can be mixed together in different combinations to create the secondary colors—green, purple, and orange. These can be further mixed to create the tertiary colors—teal, violet, and amber. My mind began tingling with the possibilities. As a person who loves creativity and systems equally, the color wheel really floats my boat.

A color wheel shows you how colors relate to each other and visually demonstrates the relationship between primary, secondary, and tertiary colors. I started to use the color wheel to develop color schemes by drawing on color theory. Once I began to understand the basics of color theory, I could see how my natural flair for color choice was actually underpinned by the pillars of color theory. It's a simple tool that can help you choose color combinations that work well together.

There are four common types of color schemes derived from the color wheel: monochromatic, analogous, complementary (and split complementary), and triadic.

The **monochromes** are the most harmonious schemes of color theory. They are formed by using a variation of shades of one color. Tone-on-tone combinations use several shades (adding black) and tints (adding white) of a single hue for a subtle palette, e.g., pastel blue, sky blue, and navy. These colors work well together naturally because their color roots are similar. Monochromatic schemes are serene and calming. Light, **pastel** tones create a relaxed, delicate feel, whereas dark **jewel** tones can feel moody and dramatic. Mixing light and dark tones adds interest and a touch of energy.

Slightly more contrasting effects can be generated by using **analogous** shades. These are colors from the same family. They sit next to one another on the color wheel; neighboring hues work well in conjunction with each other because they share the same base colors. You can choose three warm tones—such as amber, gold, and rust—to form an analogous color scheme.

Sometimes I get my inspiration from nature. After a walk once in the early spring, I noticed the eucalyptus blossoming. I came back and created an artwork using olive green and light blush pink. When I pulled out my color wheel, I realized that the reason this color combination popped so much was that it fit into the complementary scheme of color theory. **Complementary** colors—such as blue and orange, red and green, or purple and yellow—can be found on opposite sides of the color wheel. Used together, these colors appear brighter, with added *pop!* Complementary colors are guaranteed to add energy to your weave.

Colors that are not in the same color "family" or that aren't exactly harmonious can also work well together. By using a bold or deep color from one area of the color spectrum and pairing it with a lighter color from a different family, the overall impact can be quite striking. The key is to not let one color overtake the other and to keep the look balanced.

When I want a more delicate effect but with a bit of interest, **split complementary** comes to the rescue. This is a variation of the complementary color scheme: A split complementary layout is made by selecting three colors that are side by side on the color wheel and then adding the color that lies directly across the wheel from the color at the center of the trio. Not convinced? Try choosing three colors that sit adjacent on the color wheel as the base (90%) of the artwork, and the rest (10%) comes from the color that sits opposite the center of those three colors. This color scheme features less contrast, making it perfect for the less confident or the color hesitant.

The most adventurous and bold of all the schemes is the **triadic**. It is the most contrasting combination, using three hues evenly spaced on the wheel—such as turquoise, fuchsia, and yellow-orange. Triadic schemes can create a lively vibe. Use your three colors in varying shades and tints to create more contrast or soften the brightness—for instance, saturated shades of orange and turquoise, and a pastel fuchsia.

What about **neutrals**, I hear you ask? Browns, beiges, grays, black, and white form the neutral color family. They are not on the color wheel but nevertheless are very important—so important that some people weave exclusively in neutrals. Neutrals are often soft colors that allow other colors to move to the front in a design. Weavers often use neutrals for backgrounds or in other areas of the artwork they want to be less noticeable. Alternatively, a colorful background with a pop of neutral can make for a great focal point of your weave.

Use the color wheel, experiment with the basic color schemes, then let your imagination take over. Try something new. Sometimes our "mistakes" turn out to be our greatest successes. Forget about the rules you've heard about colors that do and don't match, and go with your instincts. Besides, it's more fun that way.

9

design

If you're learning to weave, there are endless tutorials across a variety of social media channels, full of smiling, helpful teachers, ready to guide you along your textile journey. They can tell you where to find your tools, what materials to buy, and even how to pack your weave for shipping. But there are not many that can help you learn how to design a piece.

Re-creating others' work is a big part of how we learn; it's a normal part of trying out your skills. But eventually you want to be able to hone in on a style that really speaks to your heart and that you can make your own. This is hard to teach, and so I came up with my own design process to help you discover your full skillset—the MM METHOD!

When I first started weaving, it felt like the Wild West. I was flailing about in a world with no rules, trying to stay alive. I found some tapestry manuals from the eighties and a few catalogs from the seventies. I mixed these up with some gusto and a lot of enthusiasm—grabbing any materials that were available to me and stuffing them into a warp. I did some . . . let's call it *interesting* work during this time (this is actually part of the origin story of the #weaveweird hashtag on Instagram).

Each piece was an opportunity to try a new skill, to jam some new materials together and cross my fingers that it would come together. I would start a piece with a fresh perspective and watch it materialize on the loom. I never had any idea how it was going to actually turn out. Often it would take a wild turn at some point in the process, and I would find myself staring at a piece that felt like I didn't even make it; it sort of "grew" on its own.

I felt out of control. Sometimes I liked it, but I could also feel so frustrated I would cry. I wanted to choose. I wanted to know how to control this unwieldy beast and when to let it run free.

My husband, who is a designer, bought me a gridded notebook and a set of Blackwing pencils. They were beautiful, but I had no idea how to use them. No one had ever taught me how to design.

Over the years I cobbled together this process, and it has been helpful in developing my own style. And I've mapped it all out here, with the hope that it can help you on your journey, too.

the MM Method

The first step in the MM Method is *finding inspiration*. Walk around with your eyes, ears, and heart open. When you start looking around with intention, you will find inspiration is everywhere. Some of my favorite sources of inspiration:

● **NATURE:** Go for a hike, swim at the beach, look into a rock pool, walk along a river, go to the park, watch the rain, or even sit in your own garden. Really be absorbed in the moment. Notice the small things. Maybe meditate, if that's your thing.

● **ART:** Take an afternoon to walk through your local galleries and museums. Go to your library and sit among the art books and leaf through them. Find some street art. Take a tour of public art in your city. Talk to artists. Join an art group.

● FASHION: Essentially art for the body. I love to see people on the street who are making a statement. Take note of color combinations, prints, shapes, proportions. Attend a fashion show. Walk around a busy neighborhood. Talk to the fashion lovers in your life.

● ARCHITECTURE: Attend open houses, stay in an Airbnb for a weekend retreat, visit cool buildings in your city (many have tours), talk to architects.

● MAGAZINES AND BOOKS: If you can't get out of your house, inspiration can be found in books and magazines, and even on Pinterest. Find an image that really speaks to you, something that maybe stimulates a memory or a moment.

I carry a sketchbook everywhere I go. You never know when inspiration will strike! If I can take five minutes in the moment when I am feeling inspired, I do the MM Method exercise. If the moment is fleeting, then I take some pics or a video on my phone and pop it into a folder called "Inspiration" so that I don't lose it. Creating a note or voice memo can be helpful, too.

The second step in the MM Method is more of an activity: Turn your sketchbook page to landscape (horizontal) and divide it into six equal sections. Each section will have a label. Take no more than 1 to 2 minutes to complete each section. This is an exercise in flow, not detail.

1 **abstract:** Can you turn the inspiration into geometric shapes? No details.

2 **magnify:** Really focus on a very small part of your inspiration. Draw what you see.

3 **repeat:** Can you find a pattern in your inspiration? If not, create one from a small detail.

4 **reflect:** Find a cool shape and create a mirror image of it.

5 **organic:** Pretend everything in front of you grew in nature. Soften the edges, and use no straight lines.

6 **quick plan:** Use the shapes and moments that have come up in the last five sections to create a 1-to-2-minute plan for a weave.

I have found that by beginning with non-fiber art inspiration, I end up creating new shapes and patterns that come from my imagination. I feel ownership of these plans more, so that I am not re-creating the work of a fellow fiber artist. When I use the MM Method, I can weave with intention. I can draw on a specific moment in time that meant something to me, and pin my art to it.

I hope the MM Method can help you feel more connected to the entire process of weaving and give you more intentional moments at the loom.

fibers

Modern weaving is all about the fibers! It is the perfect hobby for knitters, as you can use up all the excess yarn you have left over from other projects. Unlike knitting a sweater, you don't necessarily need six balls of exactly the same dye lot. It is more interesting when you use a variety of colors, types, and thicknesses.

thicker

● ROVING: Wool tops that can be pulled apart lengthwise and across the width, or used as is. They are great for texture like loops, soumak, and even rya knots. They are not spun, so there is not a lot of structural strength.

● PENCIL ROVING: Thinner wool tops, still unspun and bulkier than yarn, that really suck up color beautifully. A perfect all-arounder. Great to complete weaves quickly.

● RIBBON: Velvet, silk, chiffon. There are many beautifully hand-dyed ribbons available. They come in small lengths and are perfect for weavers. You can make your own ribbons by cutting up old clothes or sheets.

● ROPE OR CORDING: You can get cotton rope or cord in many thicknesses and colors. It comes in big cones or smaller bundles. You can also get jute, linen, and paracord. I love using rope for a thick fringe that hangs beautifully. Use a pet brush to comb out the fibers for a softer result.

● CORE-SPUN YARN: Core-spun yarn is created by twisting staple fibers around a central filament core. It is 40 to 50 percent stronger than normally spun yarn of the same weight. This style of yarn can be spun to create thick or thin fibers. Most of the core-spun yarn that I use in this book is very chunky.

mid-range

● BULKY/CHUNKY-WEIGHT YARN: Thick yarns that have some texture. I love to find "art yarn" that has been handspun. These can add interest and dimension to a woven piece.

● MEDIUM/WORSTED-WEIGHT YARN: Popular for most projects, and easily found in yarn shops and even big-box stores.

● RAFFIA/NATIVE GRASSES: Add a natural texture to a weave. Can be used in fringing and plain weave. Does not have the flexibility of yarn.

fine/super-fine/light

● LINEN: A beautiful natural fiber. Very strong. Great alternative to animal fibers.

● COTTON RUG WARP: Can be used to wrap up your projects, but also makes a great fringe. Can be used on most stitches. I like to use it for Double D locks at the beginning and end of my projects.

● SILK: I have some lovely lace-weight silk that I combine with roving to give the roving some sheen and strength. Mixing fibers can have unexpected results.

Have you thought about: silk cocoons, feathers, seed pods, dental floss, beads, crystals, leather cord…

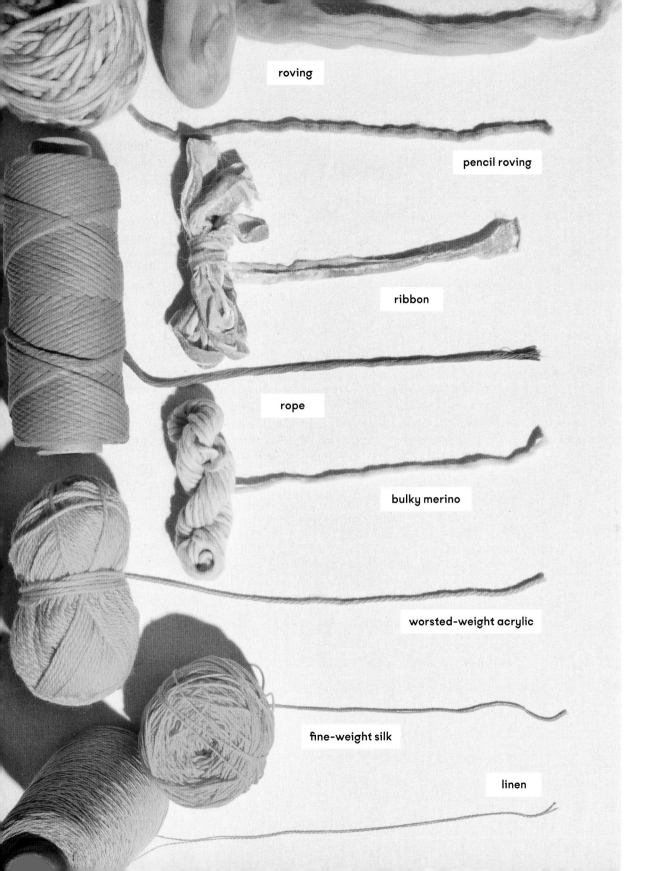

roving

pencil roving

ribbon

rope

bulky merino

worsted-weight acrylic

fine-weight silk

linen

looms

loom types

When you first begin weaving, you will need a loom. There are many different types of looms, and the type you choose will affect the style of project you can complete. I will cover a few of the simplest looms below.

CARDBOARD LOOM

One of the simplest and cheapest ways to begin weaving is to create a cardboard loom. Most of us have items delivered to our door in cardboard boxes, and so the materials for this are readily available. Simply take a rectangular piece of cardboard and use a ruler to measure out marks along two opposite sides—every ¼ inch (5 mm). Then use scissors or a utility knife (box cutter) to cut these marks about ¼ inch (5 mm) deep. Do this at both ends.

STRETCHER BAR LOOM

These are stronger and last longer than a cardboard loom. You will need to go to an art supply store and buy stretcher bars. They fit together in endless combinations to create different sizes. Use a ruler and pencil to measure out marks along two opposite sides—every ¼ inch (5 mm). Hammer small nails into the marks. If the nails seem too close together so that the wood might split, you can alternate the nails forward and back about every ¼ inch (5 mm).

WOODEN LOOM

If you have a clever woodworker among your friends or family, hit them up for a more professional loom, or trawl Etsy for one. I sell these in my Etsy shop in a variety of sizes, all professionally made using sustainable materials. They mostly come in a rectangular shape with teeth or pegs at two opposite ends. Some have a stand so that you can weave without having to hold the loom (these are my preference). If you don't have a stand, you can use an artist's easel.

CIRCLE OR SHAPED LOOM

In recent years, there have been many iterations of the shaped loom. They are a fun and easy way to create a finished woven artwork. You warp up the shape, weave your design, and then hang it, frame and all. In this book, I used some shaped looms available on Etsy.

You can do your own research into pipe looms, floor looms, backstrap looms, rigid heddle looms, tapestry looms, walking looms, and more!

loom parts and tools

Before you begin weaving, you will need to collect or make your tools. At the most basic level, you will need a loom (or something else to weave on) and a needle. Once you really get into your weaving practice, you will find that many of these other tools make weaving easier and more enjoyable, and can be immensely impactful on your body. If you are getting a sore back or neck, maybe you need to change to a weaver's sword to cut your weaving time in half. If your tension is looking a bit uneven, you could try a weaver's fork. If your arms and shoulders are getting sore from pulling the long weft through the warp, maybe you could try wrapping the tail around a shuttle. Tools can be your saving grace.

LOOM

A basic loom is rectangular in shape. It can have teeth or pegs at two opposite ends. We use these teeth to wrap our warp around. Warp and weft are the two basic components used in weaving. The lengthwise warp threads are held stationary in place on a loom while the weft is drawn through–over and under–the warp. If your loom does not have teeth, you can wrap the warp around the front and back of the loom in a circular motion and then tie the ends of the warp to the loom. You will need to move the warp into an even spacing of about ¼-inch (5 mm) increments. Make sure you tie off at the same end you started at, to ensure you have an even number of warps. If you do have teeth on your loom, tie on the first peg and then wrap the warp up and down around each corresponding tooth. Then be sure to tie off at the same end, to ensure even-numbered warps.

Make sure your warp is springy. It should vibrate when you strum your fingers across the warp. If the warp threads stick together, they are too loose. If they don't vibrate, they are too tight. It may take you a few times to figure out the correct tension. I like to lean toward a looser warp rather than tighter. It will tighten as you weave your piece, adding in weft, so if you begin with quite a loose warp you won't be battling with a tight warp for the whole piece.

WEAVER'S SWORD

This is a very handy tool to use when weaving basic, or plain, tabby weave (see page 20). After you have warped up your loom, take your weaver's sword—it looks like a flat ruler with a gently sloping end. Poke this end under the first warp and over the second warp. Then keep pushing it through the warp, weaving over and under until you get to the end.

When you turn the sword on its side, it will lift every other warp to create an opening called a shed. You can easily push your needle or shuttle loaded with weft through this shed. You close the shed by turning the weaver's sword flat.

The weaver's sword cuts your weaving time in half when creating a plain tabby. You really only need to needle-weave in one direction, and use the open shed to pass the weft in the opposite direction.

NEEDLE

I like to use a yarn needle with a big eye that can accommodate thicker fibers. Needles are best for detailed sections that you want a lot of control over. They are good when creating joins between shapes and when weaving in your ends.

SHUTTLE

Shuttles are like a thicker wooden needle but without an eye. They are a great tool for keeping a long tail in check as you weave. This means that you don't have to pull the tail through the warp, possibly damaging your weft fibers through abrasion. I use them when creating large areas of basic tabby that require a lot of fiber with not too much detail.

Hold your shuttle vertically. With your thumb, press the end of your weft fiber against the shuttle. Wind the weft fiber around the shuttle in figure 8s around either side. This helps to create a flat shuttle without too much bulk.

Now that the tail is wound away, you can use the shuttle just like a needle. Unwind the tail as you weave.

WEAVER'S FORK

A weaver's fork is a tool used to help push down your weft and create more of a dense but even weave.

After you have woven a pass of weft, you will need to bubble it to create even tension without pulling it tight. Hold the starting edge with one hand while pulling the weft up at a 45-degree angle with the other hand at the end of the shot of weft. Pull down to create a rainbow. Use the fork to push down in the middle, to create two rainbows. Then push down again in each of these to create four rainbows. Then use the fork to evenly push down each of these rainbows. This helps the weft to undulate over and under each warp thread, rather than pulling tight, and will keep your outer edges straight.

You can use a dinner fork, your fingers, or a professionally made weaver's fork, also called a **tapestry beater** or **tapestry fork**.

Other tools that can be helpful:
- CROCHET HOOK
- SCISSORS
- TAPE MEASURE
- ROTARY CUTTER
- PET BRUSH
- TAPESTRY BOBBIN
- CHOPSTICKS

stitch library

I have created a one-stop shop for the stitches in this book. Once you master these stitches, they can be mixed and matched in a number of ways to create new and exciting combinations. The really fun part of weaving comes when you begin experimenting and "finding your voice" and what you really want to say through the medium of weaving.

twining

TWINING can be used as a barrier stitch to begin and end your woven pieces. It can also be used to create a border on shapes or add texture and interest. It is a looping stitch where the weft twists around the warp threads.

Measure out at least 2 times the width of the area you want to cover. (2 times for one row of twining, 4 times for 2 rows of twining, plus a little extra for take-up, since the yarn doesn't lie in a straight line, and you need to be able to tie it at the end.) Fold the length in half. Place one tail (1) under the first warp thread; the other tail (2) will sit over. Pull until the loop is touching the warp.

Pick up tail 2 and lift it over tail 1 and then pass it behind warp thread 2. Pick up tail 1 and lift it over tail 2 and pass it behind warp thread 3. Pick up tail 2 and lift it over tail 1 and pass it behind warp thread 4. Continue along with this pattern until you get to the end. You have created a twist around each of the warps.

You can leave the twining as one pass and simply make an overhand or square knot at the end, trimming the tails. Alternatively, you can create an even stronger barrier by creating a second row of twining above the first.

To create a second row, we will continue with the tails of the first row. Take the bottom tail and pass it under the top tail and then in front of the first warp on the return trip. Take the other tail and pass it in front of the first warp thread and behind the second warp thread to secure the turn. Now you can continue the same pattern from the first row.

Knot off the end and tuck the tails between the 2 rows of twining.

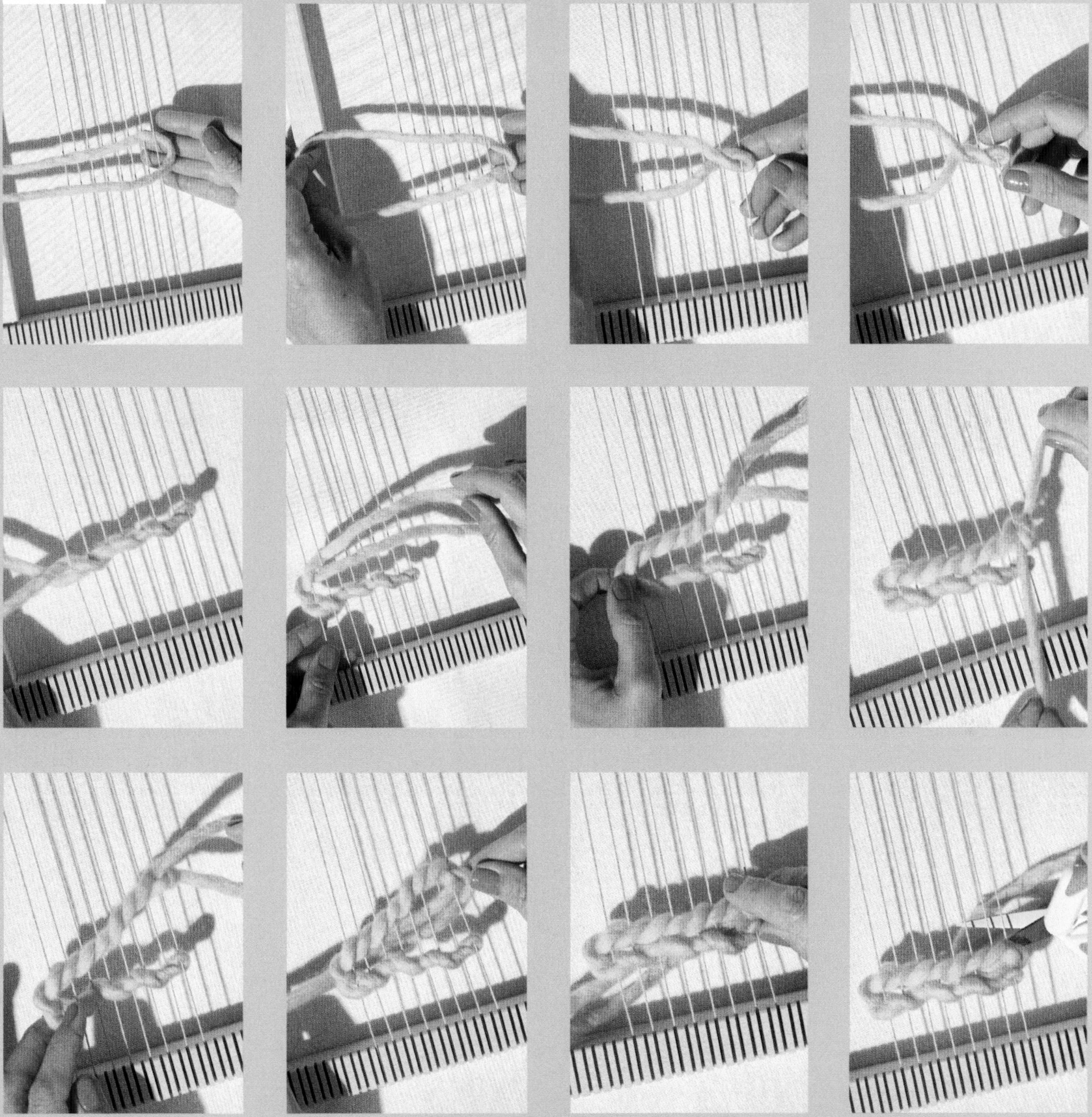

basic tabby

The most common stitch we use is usually called TABBY, though the word has another technical meaning in a different weaving application. Some people refer to it as PLAIN WEAVE. It is the bricks and mortar of any piece, creating structure and locking in other fancy stitches. It is almost always the stitch we begin and finish our work with, as well as the stitch we use to realign the warp threads after completing fancy stitches like LOOPS, SOUMAK, RYA, etc.

Thread your needle with yarn. This is called the weft. Begin by passing your threaded needle over the first warp thread and under the second, over the third and under the fourth. Continue until you come to the last warp thread. You should finish under the last. Pull the weft all the way through, leaving 2 inches (5 cm) of tail sticking out at the beginning.

If you pull the thread straight through at this point, your piece will become tight and misshapen as you weave along; this is because the weft does not travel in a straight line, but rather up and down the hills and valleys created by the warp yarns. In order to create a weave with an even structure, we must BUBBLE every pass (see below).

To weave the next row above the first, you must turn and go across in the opposite direction. If you finished over the last warp thread in the first pass of weaving, then you will begin the next row by passing under the first warp thread. Pass over and under each warp thread, checking that you are weaving the opposite to the first row. Bubble to ensure an even weave that is not pulling too tight.

Continue weaving, passing each row over one another. Once you have finished your block, you will need to weave in your ends. Turn your piece over. Take each tail in turn and thread it through the eye of a needle. Pass the needle along the second warp thread vertically back into the block of basic tabby; one will travel up the block, and the other will travel down.

bubble

Bubbling stops you from pulling too tightly across a pass of tabby. To bubble, hold the yarn at the bottom left and pull up as you weave across and then down at the end. You will notice a bump or a bubble across your weave. Push down in the middle; this will create 2 bumps or bubbles. Then push down the middle of each of these, and you end up with 4 bumps or bubbles. Now you can push these down gently using a WEAVER'S FORK (see page 17) or your fingers. Your yarn should undulate over and under the warp threads without pulling them tightly.

basket weave

BASKET WEAVE is similar to plain weave, or BASIC TABBY (see page 20). The same pattern is followed, but with two yarns combined and woven as one (the number of yarns used is even and consistent throughout).

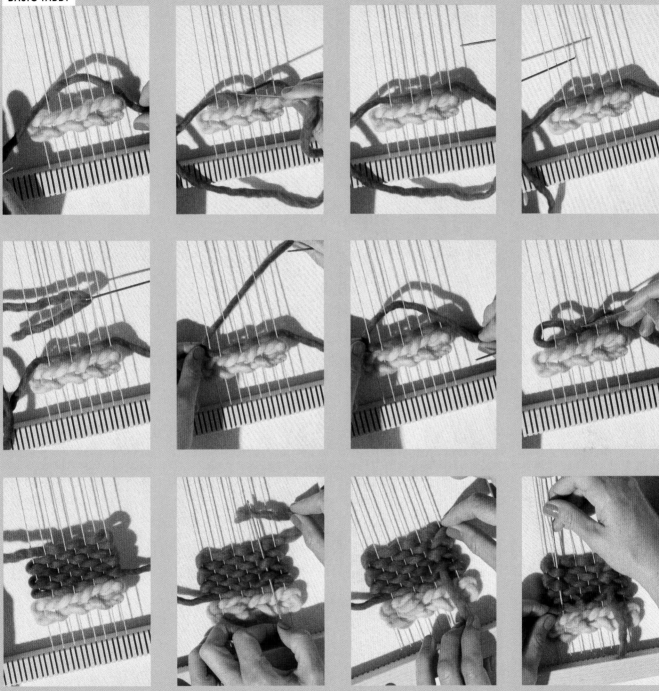

21

loops

Loops are also known as PILE WEAVE. They are a great way to add texture and dimension to a flat weave. Loops are created by manipulating a row of basic tabby by pulling some slack out every time the weft passes over a warp. They can be created using a rod to create uniform loops, or simply by pulling out some weft to create a more organic look.

Begin by weaving some basic tabby weave as a base. Take a row of tabby that is moving, for example, from left to right. Pull the weft up at a 45-degree angle. Make sure you have a little looseness in the weave.

Choose a dowel, pencil, or chopstick. The thickness of the rod you use will determine the size of your loops. Locate the first time the weft passes over the warp. Pull the weft a little and pass the dowel under the weft from top to bottom on a diagonal. Then locate the second time the weft passes over the warp. Pull the weft a little and pass the dowel under the weft from top to bottom. You will need to maneuver the dowel with your left hand while using your right to help pull the weft from right to left, creating slack. This stitch really loves to pull in at your warp, so you need to take care to give the right amount of slack by looking at your warps and making sure they remain straight and don't distort out of line.

Once you have created a row of loops, push the dowel against the block of basic tabby. Leave the dowel in place and weave 2 rows of basic tabby to lock in the stitch and reset the warp. Make sure the next row is the opposite of the loops. Push your tabby down and pull out the rod. The next row of loops will work from right to left. By weaving 2 rows of tabby between the loops, a staggered effect is reached that gives more complete coverage.

Continue this pattern of loops and tabby until you are satisfied with the result.

If you want loops to align, you will need to weave 3 rows of tabby between every row of loops. Then every row of loops will be woven in the same direction.

soumak

Soumak is another hardworking stitch that can be used to create a barrier or add texture and interest to any woven piece. When woven in two directions, it can create a braided effect. It is a looping stitch where the weft loops around the warp threads, rather than traveling in just one direction.

In this example I am doubling over my weft thread and looping the first warp on the right-hand side. I will soumak stitch on every warp. Take both tails and lift them up and over the second warp from right to left and back under from left to right. Push the weft down to close the stitch. Lift up and over the third warp from right to left and then back under from left to right. Push the soumak down toward the base block; this is referred to as BEATING, making sure the warp is covered.

Continue until you get to the last warp. Pass the weft under the last warp. Then, to create the second row, lift the weft up and over the first 2 warps from left to right. Then back under the second from right to left.

23

SOUMAK

RYA KNOTS

24

rya knots

Pull down. Lift the weft up and over the third from the left to the right warp and back under from right to left. Push down.

Weave soumak stitch all the way across the second row. When you get to the end, split the two rows of sumac and tuck the tails between and to the back. Push the rows together.

Soumak can have a different effect if you skip warps or add in more weft, or use thicker fibers like wool roving or velvet ribbon. It is a great stitch for experimentation.

Rya knots look like a TASSEL, with a knot at the top and tails hanging down. They are usually the part of a woven artwork that people want to touch. I like to save my most luxurious yarns for my rya knots, as they often draw the eye (and the hand!). They can be used in rows to create a whole shaggy weave or added to the bottom of a weave as a fringe. They can be one strand or many.

Rya knots must be bordered and locked in on both sides by basic tabby stitch. Weave a block of basic tabby and tuck in your ends.

Prepared yarn pieces should be cut before creating rya knots. You will need to employ a little math. Spool out a few yards (meters) of chosen yarn. I prefer my rya knots to be made of 4 to 6 strands per knot. You may need more if you are using thinner yarn, or fewer if you are using thicker yarn. In the example below, I am using 5 strands per rya knot.

Test the first knot to determine how many strands you will need and what their length should measure. Once you know that, you can count how many pairs of warp ends you have (since each rya knot needs 2 warp ends to tie around) and multiply the two numbers (e.g., 5 strands per knot × 10 pairs of warps = 50 strands needing to be cut). Cut those 50 strands to the desired length.

RYA KNOTS

25

Take your first group of strands and create an arc lying over your first pair of warps. Pass the tails around the outside of the warp pair and back up through the middle, between the two warp ends. Pull gently down against your basic tabby. Repeat along the row, working with the pairs of warps.

Create a second row of rya knots above the first, using a staggered pattern to fill in the gaps left from the first row.

Don't pull too tight. The knots will be locked in with rows of tabby. Weave in your ends.

knots

This is a deceptively simple stitch that adds lots of interest and texture to a weave. It's all in the preparation.

Take 5 pieces of yarn, as long as the width of your warp, measured at a 45-degree angle, plus a few inches, and lay them out together. This can be done with different yarns or kept uniform. Tie overhand knots along the length at random spacing. You can leave little loops for interest.

Use this length of knotted weft to weave basic tabby. Using a weaver's sword can be helpful to create a bigger space (shed) between warp threads, so the knots don't pull at the warps.

Pull the knots to the front and gently maneuver the weft to create the desired effect. If you want more than one row of the knotted weft effect, begin with longer pieces of yarn.

Weave your ends in.

continuous rya

This stitch can be used to create loops, much like pile weave, or cut to create a tassel effect. I love the way it is created directly from the ball, so you don't have to measure out the yarn beforehand.

KNOTS

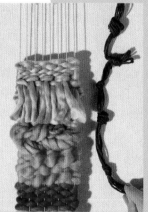   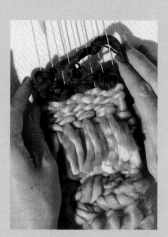

Continuous rya must be bordered and locked in on both sides by basic tabby stitch. Begin by weaving a block of basic tabby.

Pass the weft under the first warp on the left. Then create an arc lying over the second and third warps. Pass the loops over the outside of the warps and back through the middle. Pull gently to create 2 loops between the warps. Pull them gently down against your basic tabby. Take the tail and create an arc lying over the fourth and fifth warps. Pass the loops over the outside of the warps and back through the middle. Pull gently to create two loops between the warps. Pull them gently down against your basic tabby. Continue all the way along the row. Finish over the last warp.

To create a second staggered row above the first, begin by passing the tail under the first warp on the right. Then create an arc lying over the first and second warps. Pass the loops over the outside of the warps and back through the middle. Pull gently to create 2 loops between the warps. Pull them gently down against your basic tabby. Take the tail and create an arc lying over the third and fourth warps. Pass the loops over the outside of the warps and back through the middle. Pull gently to create 2 loops between the warps. Pull them gently down against your basic tabby. Continue all the way along the row.

Finish by locking in the continuous rya with a few rows of basic tabby and weaving in your ends.

lark's head knots

Fold a length of yarn in half. Place the loop over the item you're securing it to, then lift the tails and pass them through the loop. This is a LARK'S HEAD KNOT.

CONTINUOUS RYA

piecing the yarn

This is a neat little way to add extra yarn (weft) when you run out halfway through a block of tabby, without creating knots at the back of your weave.

Weave your tail toward the back and count back 3 warps from your end. Take a new length of the same fiber and begin weaving there, creating an overlap of weft on 3 warp ends. Poke the new tail toward the back. Both pieces of yarn (weft) should be woven on the same pattern of over and under. Continue weaving tabby, and no one will know the difference.

double-D lock

My friend Pauline taught me this nifty stitch that creates a strong barrier. I often use it to create a barrier at the top of my pieces between the hanging rod and the weave. You can also use this stitch to create windows of negative space in your weave. Double-D locks are created on the horizontal section of a weave.

Double-D locks can be made on single warp threads or on pairs of warps. I like to do pairs of warps when creating a barrier at the top of my weaves, as it pulls in pairs that create a loop. It looks professional and considered. In this example, I will create double-D locks on every single warp thread.

Take some binding yarn that is at least 4 times the width of the area you want to bind, and fold it in half. We will work these knots with a doubled cord throughout. Hold the loop at the bottom and lay the tail over the first warp on the right, to form the shape of a capital D. Pass the tail under the warp from left to right and through the middle of the D. Pull to close the D into a knot. Then repeat on that first warp thread, and you have tied 2 half-hitches.

Take the tail, draw it into a capital D, and lay it over the second warp. Pass it under and through the D. Repeat for a second knot on each warp (hence the double-D).

Move across to the third warp and repeat. Continue all the way across the warp, creating double-D locks until you reach the end. If you have any tail left over, weave a few rows of basic tabby.

The first time you try this, it won't look perfect, but it's easy to take out and redo. After you do it on 20 or 30 warp ends, it will look just fine, I promise. It's also easier looking at the photos as you go.

passementerie

Take 2 yards (2 m) of core-spun bulky yarn. Lay this in the opposite shed from the last row of tabby. Leave about 1 inch (2.5 cm) to the beginning of the row on the right side, and the rest will lie to the left, awaiting its turn after the next section of tabby. Now take 4 yards (4 m) of another color for the second section of tabby. Follow the steps to create another section of tabby. Make sure that the first row of this section is on the opposite shed to the passementerie thread. Once you have woven to the end of the section of tabby, pick up the long length of passementerie yarn and lay it in above the section of tabby. Be sure to leave a loop of thread billowing out beyond the last warp thread. This will create an intricate edge.

PIECING THE YARN

PASSEMENTERIE

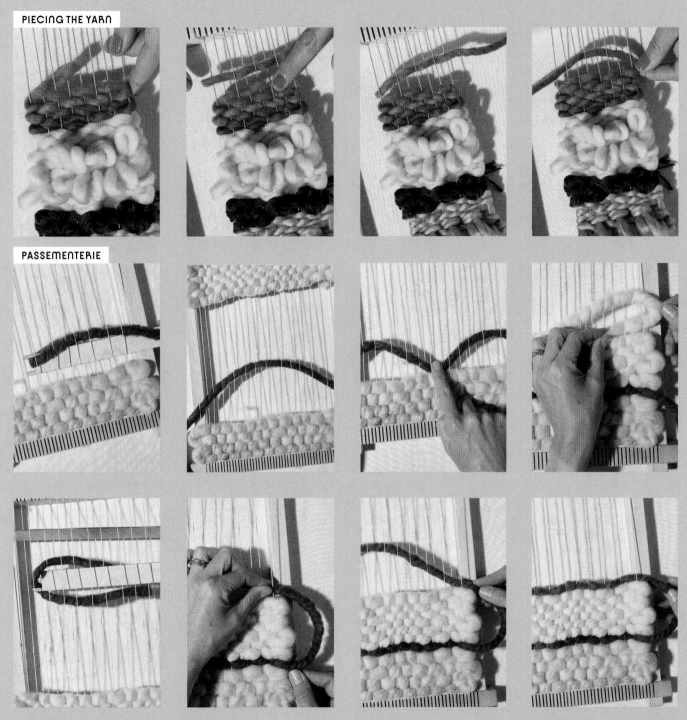

29

dovetail

Take your first color and work basic tabby from the left side toward the middle. Do not weave all the way across. Choose a warp (let's call it the DOVETAIL WARP) and turn around on that warp and weave back to the left side. Then pick up a second color and weave from the right side to the dovetail warp, and turn around on that warp and weave back to the right side. Pick up your first color on the left and weave back to the dovetail warp, and turn around on that warp and weave back to the left. Then pick up your second color and weave from the right to the dovetail warp, and turn around on that warp and weave back to the right. Note: Both colors are turning around on the same warp. This creates a join between the two colors and a lovely inlay pattern. Continue weaving this dovetail-joined weave, packing the wefts tightly together by pushing your weave down against the cardboard. Weave in your ends.

twill

TWILL can be identified by its pattern of diagonal lines. It is formed by passing the weft yarn under and over multiple warp yarns, in an alternating sequence that creates a diagonal ribbed pattern on the woven surface. You can expand this pattern to fit your amount of warps.

tassels

Tassels can be made in any size and color, and are an excellent accessory to many project. Select your color and yarn choice, cut the cotton into 6 lengths of the same size, and hold them together in a bundle. Fold the bundle in half and pull the tails to the same length. The yarns in this bundle need to be secured by wrapping them in place. Take 1 yard (1 m) of colored cotton to wrap these in place. Lay the beginning of the colored cotton along the section, and wrap over the top of the tail. Be sure that each wrap sits exactly next to the last wrap, and thread the ending tail into a needle to secure the ends back under the wraps.

batch weaving

BATCH WEAVING is weaving more than one piece at the same time on the same warp. Warping and setting up your loom can be time consuming. Batch weaving can streamline your weaving by setting up your loom once to create many of the same project.

DOVETAIL

TASSELS

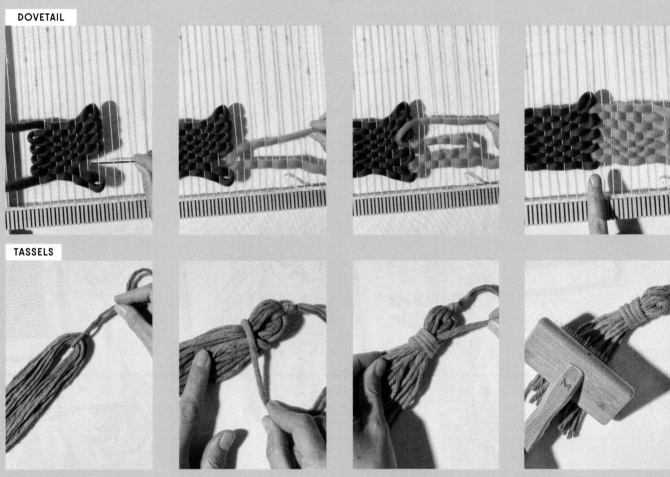

PROJECTS

BEGINNER

34

INTERMEDIATE

80

ADVANCED

138

● begi nner

fluffy shag rya weaving

MATERIALS

12 × 18-inch (30 × 46 cm) loom or cardboard loom

15 yards (14 m) cotton rug warp

yarn in five different jewel tones, about 10 yards (10 m) of each

scissors

yarn needle or shuttle

weaver's fork (optional)

12-inch (30 cm) dowel or rod for hanging

COLOR STORY

jewel-toned rainbow

TECHNIQUES

basic tabby, bubble, rya knots

35

METHOD

1

Warp up your loom. Tie your cotton rug warp on the top left peg and then draw it down to the bottom-left peg, around and back up and around the second peg on the top left. Continue all the way along from left to right across your loom until you reach the last, top-right peg. Wrap the warp thread around the last peg 2 times, but do not tie off yet. You'll want to check your tension, and you may need to readjust.

2

Check your warp for even and correct tension. It should be springy and even all the way across. It should strum and vibrate when you pass your fingers across the warp threads. If the warp threads stick together, it is too loose. Correct the tension, and when you are happy with it, tie off on the top-right peg.

3

Thread your needle with about 4 yards (4 m) of your first color (if you want to weave faster, or if you are using thinner yarn, you can double your yarn). This is your weft. Begin weaving BASIC TABBY (see page 20) at the bottom left across to the right. Basic tabby goes over and under, over and under all the way across. It doesn't really matter if you begin over or under.

4

Be sure to BUBBLE each row (see page 20) to ensure you are getting even tension.

5

When you get to the end of your first row, turn back and weave your second row directly above, from right to left. This row or pass should be the opposite of the first row. Be sure to bubble. Check that your ends are touching the first and last warps without bagging or pulling in.

6

Continue weaving until the yarn runs out. Weave the ends in by turning back in on the weave; weave the opposite to the row above or below and then vertically back into the color you were just weaving. This will tuck the tail into the weave without its being visible from the front.

7

You have just woven the header of your piece. We are weaving upside down, from the top of the piece up to the bottom. By doing it this way, we are left with a nice, neat top to the weaving, with the loops already created using the warp threads.

8

Now you will weave your first row of RYA KNOTS (see page 25). You will need to cut about 5 or 6 lengths of yarn for each rya, using the same color as the header. The length of the pile that you cut will determine the length of your fringe. I made my lengths by winding yarn around a small, slim paperback book, approximately 5 inches (13 cm) wide, so the lengths are 11 inches (28 cm). We need them slightly longer, as we are going to cut them into a zigzag pattern once the weaving is complete.

9

Take one bunch of 5 or 6 lengths and fold them in half, like a smile or the letter U. Lay this U across your first 2 warps on the left side of your weave. Pass the left side of the U ends under the first warp thread and back up between the first and the second warps. Then pass the right side of the U ends under the second warp and back up between the first and second warps. Pull up the ends and lay them flat across the top of your rya knot. You have completed your first rya knot. Continue across the weave, tying knots on each pair of warp threads until you have completed the entire row.

10

Once you have completed your row of rya, you will need to lock it in with rows of basic tabby, using the same color as the header.

11

To do this, repeat steps 3 to 6 to create another block of basic tabby. Weave your ends in as you go.

12

Add a second color of rya. We are creating a layered fringe on this piece, so you can go monochromatic or get wild with different colors for each layer. You can use different types and colors of yarn to add texture to your piece. Follow steps 8 to 10 to create your row of rya knots. You can change length to add interest and dimension.

13

Lock in your second row of rya by repeating steps 3 to 6, using the second color.

39

14

Continue along, following the pattern—block of basic tabby/row of rya knots/block of basic tabby—until you are happy with your piece. Change color with each block. I made the last row of rya slightly longer.

15

Finish off your weaving with 3 to 4 rows of tabby to secure your piece.

16

Trim the layers of rya into a zigzag.

17

To remove the work, pull the warp loops off the top of your loom (the bottom of the weaving) and tie some knots in the warp, to hold the weaving where you want it to stay, remembering that this will be hidden by the last row of fringe.

18

One of the most satisfying parts of weaving is hanging your completed piece. On the opposite side of the piece, pop the warp loops off the loom, passing a rod (or branch, or spoon—experiment!) through your loops until all the loops are on the rod you will hang the piece from. Be sure to pass the rod through opposite to the last row of tabby that you did. To hang the rod, tie a piece of yarn to each end. Lift up your weaving and admire your work!

braided soumak weaving

12 × 18-inch (30 × 46 cm) loom

15 yards (14 m) cotton rug warp

super-chunky yarn in 8 pastel rainbow tones, 4 yards (4 m) of each; I used Roving Textiles Superfluff

Merino wool roving in 6 pastel tones, 1 yard (1 m) of each

33 yards (30 m) cotton cord; I used Cloud 9 Macrame String from Mary Maker Studio, in Rosewater

scissors

yarn needle or shuttle

12-inch (30 cm) dowel or rod for hanging

~~~~~

COLOR STORY
rainbow pastel

TECHNIQUES
basic tabby, bubble, soumak

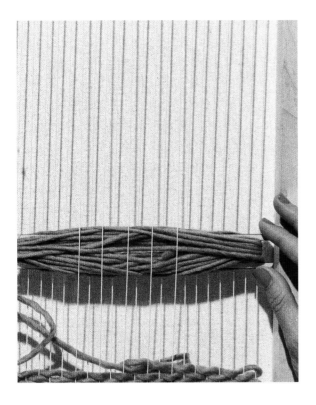

1

Warp up your loom. Tie your cotton rug warp on the top left peg and then draw it down to the bottom-left peg, around, and back up and around the second peg on the top left. Continue all the way along from left to right across your loom until you reach the last, top-right peg. Wrap the warp thread around the last peg 2 times, but do not tie off yet. You want to check your tension, and you may need to readjust.

2

Check your warp for even and correct tension. It should be springy and even all the way across, and should strum and vibrate when you pass your fingers across the warp threads. If the warp threads stick together, it is too loose. Correct the tension, and when you are happy with it, tie off on the top-right peg.

3

Thread your needle with about 4 yards (4 m) of one color of yarn. This is the weft. Begin weaving BASIC TABBY (see page 20), starting at the bottom left and working across to the right. Basic tabby goes over and under, over and under all the way across. It doesn't really matter if you begin over or under.

4

Be sure to BUBBLE each row (see page 20) to ensure you are getting even tension all the way up your weave. It stops you from pulling too tightly across a pass of tabby.

5

When you get to the end of your first row, turn back and weave your second row directly above, from right to left. This row or pass should be the opposite of the first row. Be sure to bubble. Check that your ends are touching the first and last warps without bagging or pulling in.

43

 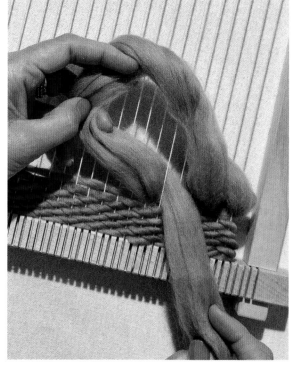

6

Continue weaving until the yarn runs out. I wove 16 rows. Weave in the ends by turning back in on the weave; weave the opposite to the row above or below and then vertically back into the color you were just weaving. This will tuck the tail into the weave without its being visible from the front.

7

You have just woven the header of your piece. We are weaving upside down, from the top of the piece up to the bottom. By doing it this way, we are left with a nice, neat top to the weaving, with the hanger loops already created using the warp threads.

8

Now you will weave your first row of SOUMAK (see page 22). Soumak is a looping stitch where the weft (yarn) loops around the warp threads to create a braided look. The braid is created in two parts. We create a single row of sumac stitch in one direction and then turn back and reverse the soumak for a second row. Start with a length of yarn at least 4 times as long as the loom is wide. I am using 1½ yards (1.5 m) of wool roving. This is quite a thick fiber, and I want a really voluminous look. Beginning on the left, pass your tail under the first warp thread and back over the second warp thread and push to the back. This will tuck the tail away. Now you have a long piece of yarn to work with. Wrap the yarn up over the first warp and second warp thread. Then pass the yarn under the second warp so that it comes up between the first and second warp thread. Make sure that the end of the yarn is pulling *downward, under itself,* and not upward. Don't pull too tightly. Allow the weft to move around the warp without pulling. You may want to pull the looped stitch into place to sit nicely. You have completed your first soumak stitch. Move 2 warp threads over to the

45

right, and wrap the yarn around the second thread of this new set and up between the 2 warps, pulling *downward*. Continue these steps, moving toward the right, until you have completed your row. There should be 2 warp threads left at the end of the row. Simply pass the yarn under the last warp; this will help you turn around for the next 2 rows of soumak.

9

I chose a second color of wool roving to reverse the soumak. Reverse your soumak for a second row to create a braided look. To reverse your stitch, cross over the warp thread to the left of your last warp thread, and loop behind that thread, coming up between it and the last warp thread. Be sure that your yarn is pulling *downward*. This will create the opposite side of the braid.

10

Cover 2 new warp threads with your yarn, looping around the second thread of the set. Be sure that you loop and pull *downward*. Continue these steps, moving toward the left, until you have completed your row. Soumak all the way across, including the last pair of the row.

11

Split the 2 rows of soumak apart slightly, and tuck the ends in between the rows to hide them.

12

Once you have completed your soumak, you will need to lock it in with rows of basic tabby. To do this, repeat steps 3 to 6 to create another block. Choose a new color of pastel super-chunky yarn. Weave in the ends as you go.

13

Add a second soumak braid, using 2 new colors of wool roving to complete the two sides of the braided soumak. Follow steps 8 to 11 to create your second braid.

14

Lock in your second row of soumak, following steps 3 to 6. Choose a new color of pastel yarn.

15

Continue along, following the pattern—block of basic tabby/soumak braid/block of basic tabby—until you are happy with your piece. I wove 4 sets.

16

Now we are going to add a layer of RYA KNOTS (see page 25) to make fringe. You will need to cut about 4 lengths of yarn for each rya. I used cotton cord. The length of the pile that you cut will determine the length of your fringe. I made my lengths by winding yarn around a book, so my lengths were approximately 12 inches (30 cm).

17

Take one bunch of 4 lengths and fold them in half like a smile or a U. Lay this U across your first two warps on the left-hand side of your weave. Pass the left side of the U ends under the first warp thread and back up between the first and the second warps. Then pass the right-hand side of the U ends under the second warp and back up between the first and second warps. Pull up the eight ends and lay them flat across the top of your rya knot. You have completed your first rya knot.

18

Continue across the weave, tying knots on each pair of warp threads until you have completed the entire row.

19

Finish your weaving off with 3 or 4 rows of tabby to secure your piece. This will sit under the fringe of rya knots, so you can use any yarn you have on hand.

20

To remove the work, pull the warp loops off your loom and tie some knots in the warp close to the bottom of the weaving (that's the end you just finished; remember, we are weaving from the top of the piece to the bottom) to hold the weaving where you want it to stay.

21

One of the most satisfying parts of weaving is hanging your completed piece. Just as you did at the bottom of your weaving, you can pop the warp loops off their pegs at the top (this is where you started weaving). As you go, pass a rod (or branch, or spoon—experiment!) through your loops until all the loops are on the rod. Be sure to pass the rod through opposite to the last row of tabby that you did. To hang the rod, tie a piece of yarn to each end. Lift up your weaving and admire your work!

color gradation bookmark

COLOR STORY

complementary
pastels—mint, lilac

TECHNIQUES

basic tabby, bubble,
twining

MATERIALS

12 × 18-inch (30 × 46 cm) loom or cardboard loom

4 yards (4 m) cotton rug warp or cord

embroidery floss: 87 yards (80 m) in mint green; 70 yards (64 m) in lilac

cardboard spacer

scissors

yarn needle or shuttle

weaver's fork (optional)

Through
the Eyes
of Friends

paper
52.8 cm

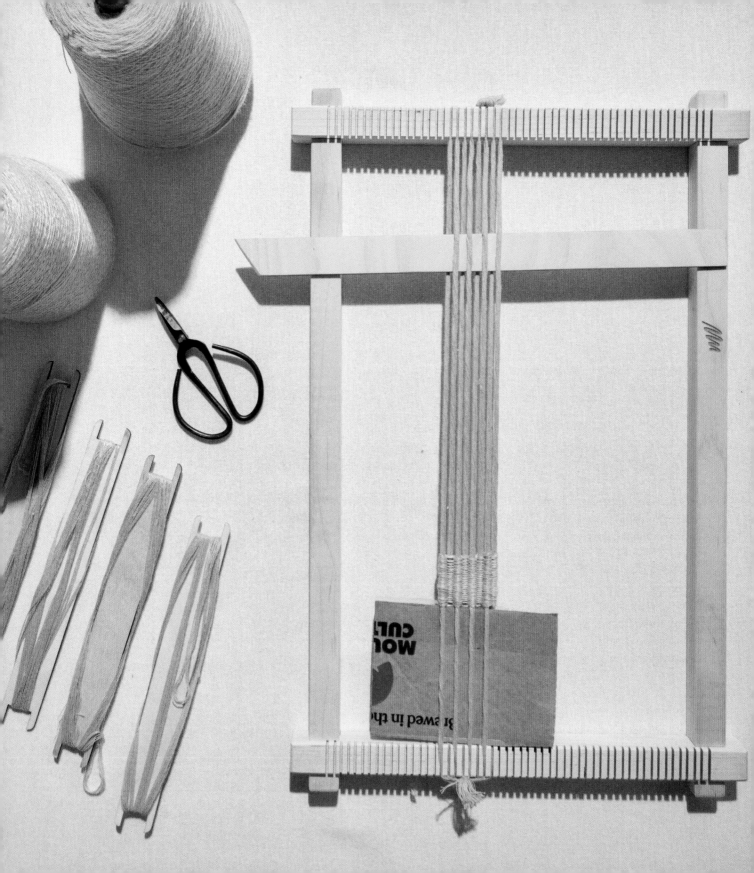

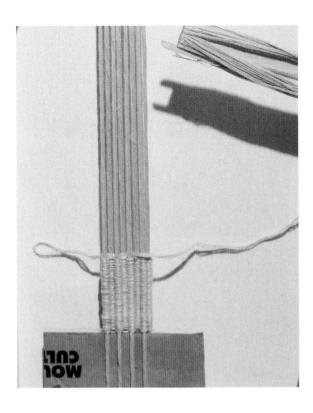

when you are happy with it, tie off on the top-right peg. Weave your cardboard spacer across the bottom, to allow enough room for fringe.

3

First you need to prepare your yarns. These will be the weft. I chose very fine embroidery cotton or lace-weight yarn in mint. You will need 4 lengths of 4 yards (4 m) each. These will all be held together as one. Thread your needle or load your shuttle with the four lengths. Begin weaving BASIC TABBY (see page 20) at the bottom left across to the right. Check that the knots that secure your warp to the loom are at the opposite end. Basic tabby goes over and under, over and under all the way across. It doesn't really matter if you begin over or under.

4

Be sure to BUBBLE each row (see page 20) to ensure you are getting even tension all the way up your weave.

5

When you get to the end of your first row, turn back and weave your second row directly above from right to left. This row or pass should be the opposite of the first row. Be sure to bubble. Check that your ends are touching the first and last warps without bagging or pulling in.

6

Continue weaving until the yarn runs out. I wove 30 rows. Weave your ends in by turning back in on the weave, weave the opposite to the row above or below and then vertically back into the color you were just weaving. This will tuck the tail into the weave without seeing it from the front.

7

You have just woven the topmost basic tabby section of your piece. We are weaving upside down from the top of the piece up to the bottom.

1

Warp up your loom with the cotton rug warp. We will only be warping up a small section of the loom: A bookmark is usually about 8 to 10 warps wide. Tie your warp on the top-left peg and then draw it down to the bottom-left peg, around, and back up and around the second peg on the top left. Continue along from left to right across your loom until you have 8 or 10 warps across, ending at the top-right peg. Wrap the warp thread around the last peg 2 times, but do not tie off yet. You want to check your tension, and you may need to readjust.

2

Check your warp for even and correct tension. It should be springy and even all the way across, and should strum and vibrate when you pass your fingers across the warp threads. If the warp threads stick together, it is too loose. Correct the tension, and

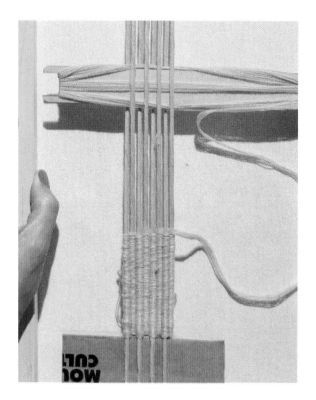
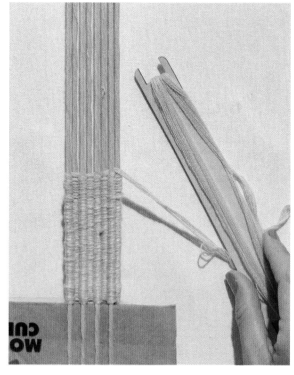

8

Now we will begin to grade to our next color in the second section of basic tabby. I chose lilac as my second color. Prepare your yarns. I used three lengths of mint and one length of lilac for a ratio of 3:1. Measure 4 yards (4 m) of each. Follow steps 3 to 6 to create another section of tabby.

9

For the third section of basic tabby you will need 2 lengths of mint and 2 lengths of lilac, for a ratio of 2:2. Cut 4 yards (4 m) of each. Follow steps 3 to 6 to create another section of tabby.

10

For the fourth section of basic tabby you will need 1 length of mint and 3 lengths of lilac, for a ratio of 1:3. Cut 4 yards (4 m) of each. Follow steps 3 to 6 to create another section of tabby.

11

For the fifth section of basic tabby you will need 4 lengths of lilac, cut to 4 yards (4 m) each. Follow steps 3 to 6 to create another section of tabby.

12

Bind off the ends so the weaving doesn't slip off the warp. There are a variety of binding stitches—TWINING is a good one (see page 18).

13

Repeat the binding on the other end of the bookmark, removing the spacer.

14

Cut the end loops and trim to the desired length.

15

Comb or brush out the thick cord warp to create tassels at both ends. Be sure to hold the weaving in place as you brush.

loopy bubble weaving

~~~

neutral tones of cream and gray

TECHNIQUES

twining, basic tabby, bubble, loops, rya

MATERIALS

12 × 18-inch (30 × 46 cm) loom or cardboard loom

6 yards (5.5 m) each of Echoview Fiber Mill Rug chunky yarn in Hedwig and Chickadee

2 yards (2 m) each of Roving Textiles roving in Sand and Milk

16 yards (14.5 m) of cotton rug warp

scissors

yarn needle or shuttle

weaver's sword

12-inch dowel or rod for loops and hanging

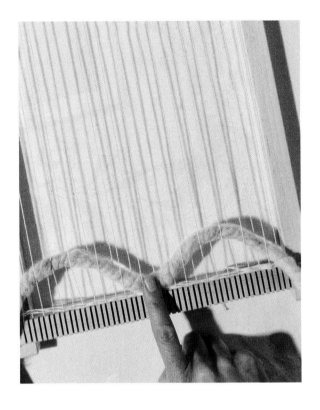

METHOD

1

Warp up your loom. Tie your cotton rug warp on the top-left peg and then draw it down to the bottom-left peg, around, and back up and around the second peg on the top left. Continue all the way along, moving from left to right across your loom until you reach the last, top-right peg. Wrap the warp thread around the last peg 2 times, but do not tie off yet. You want to check your tension, and you may need to readjust.

2

Check your warp for even and correct tension. It should be springy and even all the way across, and should strum and vibrate when you pass your fingers across the warp threads. If the warp threads stick together, it is too loose. Correct the tension, and when you are happy with it, tie it off on the top-right peg. Weave in your weaver's sword.

3

Create a border at the top of your weave by weaving 2 rows of TWINING (see page 18). I used the same cotton I used for warp for this border. Measure out 6 times the width of the loom. Fold the yarn in half and pass one half behind the first warp on the right. Take the thread that is over the first warp and pass it under the second warp. Then pick up the thread that is over the second warp and pass it under the third warp. Continue twining all the way across the loom, and turn it around for ease in twining back in the other direction for the second row.

55

4

Thread your needle or load your shuttle with about about 6 yards (6 m) of your first color. This is your weft. Begin weaving BASIC TABBY (see page 20) starting from the bottom left and working across to the right. Check that the beginning and ending knots fastening your warp to the loom are at the opposite end of the loom from where you are starting. Basic tabby goes over and under, over and under, all the way across. It doesn't really matter if you begin over or under.

5

Be sure to BUBBLE each row of weft (see page 20) to ensure you are getting even tension all the way up your weave.

6

When you get to the end of your first row, turn back and weave your second row directly above from right to left. This row or pass should be the opposite of the first row; the under and the over switch. Be sure to bubble. Check that your ends are touching the first and last warps without bagging or pulling in.

7

Continue weaving until the yarn runs out—I wove 20 rows. Weave in your ends by turning back in on the weave; weave the opposite to the row above or below and then vertically back into the color you were just weaving. This will tuck the tail into the weave without its being visible from the front.

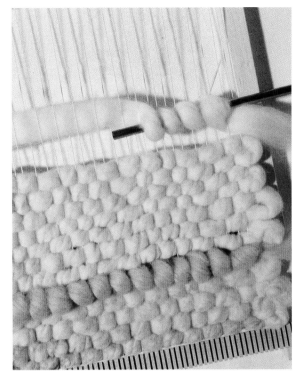

8

You have just woven the header of your piece. We are weaving upside down, from the top of the piece up to the bottom. By doing it this way, we are left with a nice, neat top to the weaving, with the loops already created using the warp threads.

9

Now you will weave your first row of LOOPS (see page 22). Measure out 2 yards (2 m) of roving. Separate the roving lengthwise into thirds. This will make it less chunky. In order to create a row of loops, we need to first weave a row of tabby, and then we will manipulate this row of tabby over a rod to create loops. Once you have woven a row of tabby, tuck the starting tail into the weaving block below to anchor the new fiber. Take your dowel and pop it under and through the first weft that goes over a warp. You may need to pull a little more slack to incorporate the dowel. Then pop it under and through the weft as it

passes over the second warp. Again, pull a little slack to incorporate the dowel. Continue along, passing the dowel under and through, every time the weft passes *over* a warp. Once you have finished the row, keep the dowel in place. Wrap the roving tail around to the back of the piece and tuck back into the roving wefts.

10

Take your next color of roving and measure out 6 yards (6 m). Weave 2 rows of basic tabby above the roving loops to secure the loops before slipping the dowel out. Then push the tabby rows down to hold the loops in place. Continue weaving until you run out of yarn.

11

Continue along, following the pattern—block of basic tabby/row of loops/block of basic tabby—until you are happy with your piece.

57

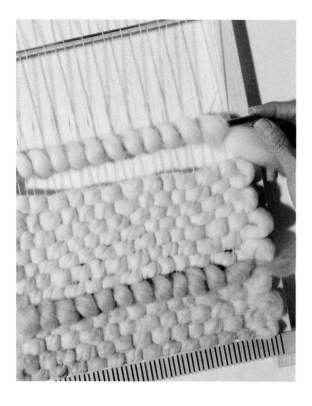

12

Now we are going to add a layer of RYA KNOTS (see page 25). You will need to cut a few lengths of yarn for each rya knot. The length of the pile that you cut will determine the length of your fringe. I wanted a long fringe, so I made my lengths by winding yarn around a book—approximately 20 inches (50 cm). When folded in half, they measured 10 inches (25 cm), so the fringe is 10 inches (25 cm) long.

13

Take one bunch of lengths and fold them in half like a smile or the letter U. Lay this U across your first 2 warps on the left side of your weave. Pass the left side of the U ends under the first warp thread and back up between the first and second warps. Then pass the right side of the U ends under the second warp and back up between the first and second warps. Pull up the 2 (bunches of) ends and lay them flat across the top of your rya knot. You have completed your first rya knot. Continue across the weave, tying knots on each pair of warp threads until you have completed the entire row.

14

Finish off your weaving with 3 or 4 rows of tabby to secure your piece. This will sit under the fringe of rya knots (remember, you are weaving upside down, from the top of the piece to the bottom), so you can use any yarn you have on hand; it won't show.

15

Then simply cut the warp threads off your loom at that end, and tie knots in adjacent pairs of warps close to the bottom of the weaving, to hold the weaving where you want it to stay.

16

One of the most satisfying parts of weaving is hanging your completed piece. Unlike what you did at the bottom of your weaving, you can just pop the warp loops off their pegs at the top. As you go, pass a rod (or branch, or spoon—experiment!) through your loops until all the loops are on the rod. Be sure to pass the rod through opposite to the last row of tabby that you did; that is, go under the overs, and over the unders. To hang the rod, tie a piece of yarn to each end. Lift up your weaving and admire your work!

5 yards (5 m) natural-colored cotton rope or cording

6 yards (6 m) of cotton warps or thinner cotton yarn each in red, rose, coral, gold, mustard, lime, green, aqua, denim, navy, and purple

scissors

yarn needle

hooks or dowels for hanging

tassel rainbow bunting

COLOR STORY
bright rainbow with a neutral border

TECHNIQUES
tassels

1

Measure out and cut the length of your 5-yard (5 m) cotton rope to the length you require for the bunting. I used about 1½ yards (1.5 m).

2

First we want to create loops at each end to hang our bunting. Wrap one end around your finger and back along the rope. Take about 1 yard (1 m) of colored cotton to wrap these in place. Lay the end of the colored cotton along this section, and wrap over the top of these tails. Be sure that each wrap sits exactly next to the last wrap.

3

Once you have wrapped the end in place, take the needle and thread the end back through and underneath the wrap. Snip off any extra cotton. Repeat on the other end of the rope.

4

Now we will create our first tassel. Cut the neutral cotton into 6 lengths of the same size and hold them together in a bundle. Mine were quite short (about 4 inches/10 cm), but you can make these longer.

5

Fold the bundle over the rope, and pull the tails to the same length. We need to secure the yarns in this bundle by wrapping them in place. Take 1 yard (1 m) of colored cotton to wrap these in place. Lay the beginning of the colored cotton along the section, and wrap over the top of the tail. Be sure that each wrap sits exactly next to the last wrap, and thread the ending tail into a needle to secure the ends back under the wraps.

6

Repeat this tassel process along the length of the rope. I used a rainbow gradation, including gold, to bind the tassels in place.

circle roving hoop hanging

~~~

COLOR STORY
neutral

TECHNIQUES
**lark's head knots,
basic tabby**

**8 to 10 yards (8 to 10 m) of
neutral-colored roving**

brass macramé hoop

scissors

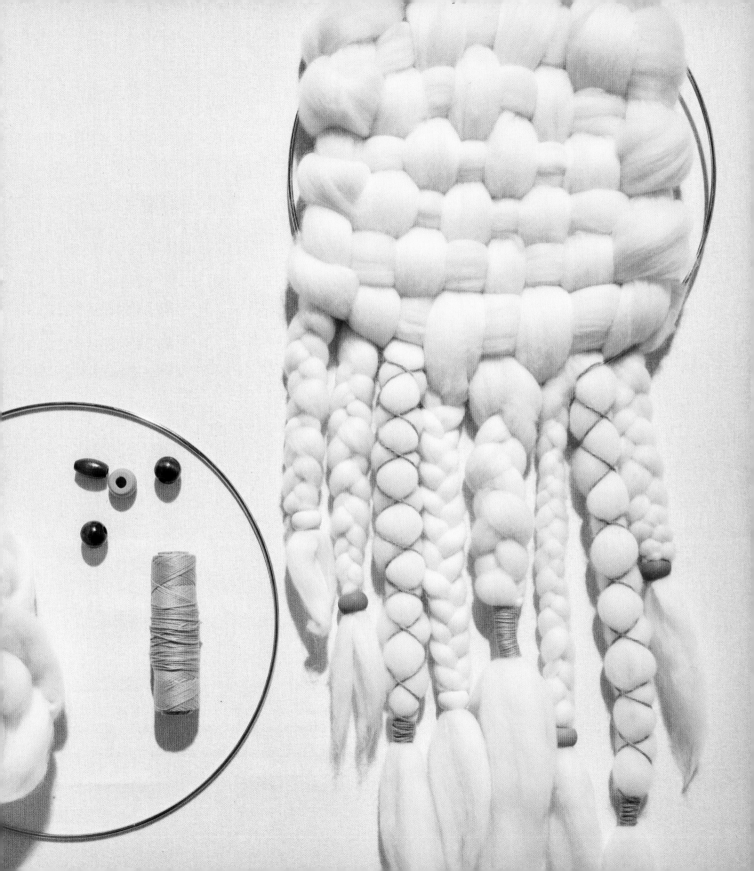

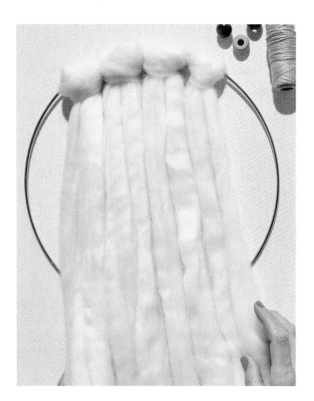
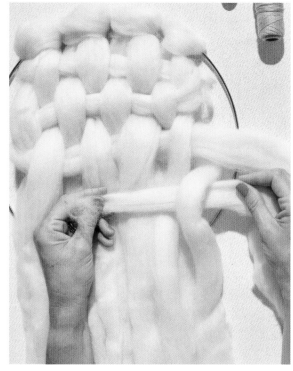

1

Measure out 4 lengths of your roving, 1 yard (1 m) each, and pull apart or cut. These will form your warp (the vertical fiber you weave on). You should end up with about 3 to 4 yards (3 to 4 m) of roving left over. This will be used as your weft (the fiber that will pass horizontally over and under the warp).

2

First we need to take our strips and create LARK'S HEAD KNOTS (see page 27) to secure them to the hoop. Create knots with all 4 strips, until you have 4 lark's head knots and 8 tails hanging down.

3

Take the long length of roving. We are about to weave on our tails (warp) using BASIC TABBY (see page 20). First secure the end of the long strip by tying a knot on the first tail (warp) on the left side.

4

Now take the long end and pass it over the first tail on the left-hand side of the hoop. Then pass it under the next tail directly to the right. Continue passing over and under in plain weave until you have reached the right-hand side of the tails (warp). Make sure this row of weaving is as close to the top of the weaving (where the lark's heads knots are) as possible. Don't pull too tightly; this looks best when it's slightly puffy and soft.

5

Weave another row of basic tabby below the first. This row needs to be the opposite of the first row. In the first row, we went *under* the last tail. And so we need to begin the second row moving right to left and go *over* the first warp tail.

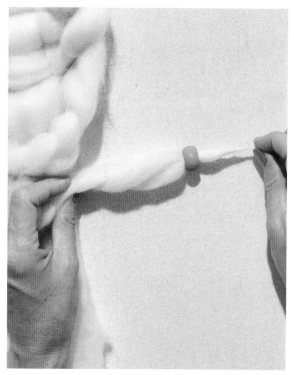

6

Continue moving over and under the tails (warp) and back and forth on each row until you have filled up the hoop. Make sure the last row of tabby sits nice and snug against the brass hoop at the bottom.

7

You can add a bit of textural interest by adding a thinner roving braid or two to the fringe. Simply split a length of roving lengthwise into 3 sections. Tie a knot to secure it to the back of the woven section. Braid the 3 sections together and secure with a bead (this will be easier to thread with a crochet hook) or by wrapping the end with cotton yarn to secure it.

mini framed weaving

12 × 18-inch (30 × 46 cm) loom or cardboard loom

11 yards (10 m) of cotton rug warp

6 yards (6 m) of yarn; I used a variety of thick and thin yarns and fibers, about 1 yard (1 m) of each in six different colors

scissors

yarn needle or shuttle

cardboard spacer

weaver's fork (optional)

double-sided tape or PVA glue

frame (preferably a shadow box frame with the glass removed)

COLOR STORY
monotone greens/
monotone naturals

TECHNIQUES
basic tabby, bubble

1

Pull the frame apart. You should find the following:

- frame
- glazing (glass—we won't be using this; please recycle where possible or reuse)
- mat (card with a hole in the middle to see the artwork)
- a backing paper that your weaving will stick to (if it has a picture, simply turn it over to the blank side)
- backing board and the hardware on the back to stand or hang

2

Measure out the area of your required weaving on the frame. I made mine slightly smaller than the hole in the mat.

3

Use cotton rug warp to warp up your loom. The width of your warp will depend on the size of your mat's opening. You don't need to warp up the whole width of the loom; you can warp up only the middle section. Tie your cotton rug warp on the top-left peg and then draw it down to the bottom-left peg, around, and back up and around the second peg on the top left. Continue along from left to right across your loom until you reach the required width. Check that you have correct tension and then tie off on the top-right peg.

4

Weave in the cardboard spacer along the bottom of the warp. Weave over and under each warp thread in the usual plain weave. This will center your weave and give you space in the warp to tie off the warp at the end.

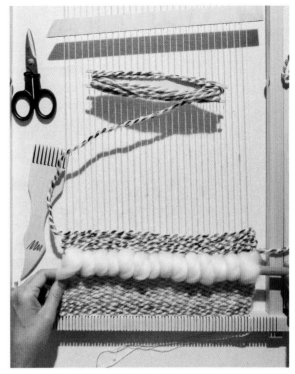

5
Prepare your fibers and yarns. Cut about 1 yard (1 m) of each fiber or yarn. We will weave each section of BASIC TABBY (see page 20) in turn. This is your weft.

6
Thread your needle with the first yarn of your choice. Begin weaving basic tabby at the bottom left across to the right. Basic tabby goes over and under, over and under, all the way across. It doesn't really matter if you begin over or under.

7
Be sure to BUBBLE each row (see page 20) to ensure you are getting even tension all the way up your weave.

8
When you get to the end of your first row, turn back and weave your second row directly above, from right to left. This row or pass should be the opposite of the first row. Be sure to bubble. Check that your ends are touching the first and last warps without bagging or pulling in.

9
Continue weaving until the yarn runs out. I wove 5 rows. Weave in your ends by turning back in on the weave; weave the opposite to the row above or below and then vertically back into the color you were just weaving. This will tuck the tail into the weave without its being visible from the front.

10
You have just woven the first tabby section of your piece.

69

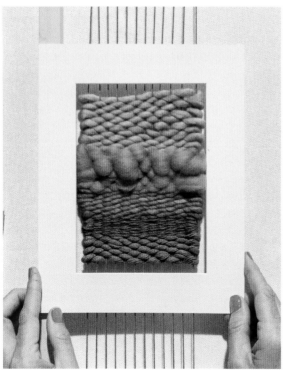

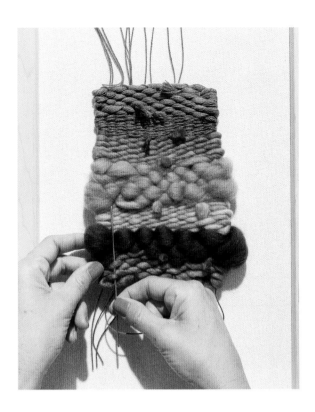

11

Take your second fiber and repeat steps
5 to 7.

12

Repeat steps 6 to 9 with each fiber, continuing to check with the mat measurements to ensure your woven piece will sit nicely inside the frame.

13

Once you are happy with the size of your piece, it's time to take it off the loom. Simply cut the warp loops off your loom and tie knots in the warp close to the bottom and top of the weaving, to hold the weaving where you want it to stay. Knotting each pair of adjacent warp ends is probably the easiest way to do this.

14

Turn the weave over and weave each warp end back into the weaving vertically.

15

Take your backing paper from the frame and lay the weave in place. Take the weave off and apply your adhesive to the backing paper of the frame where the weave will go. Either double-sided tape or PVA glue works well. Lay your weave over the top and press down to ensure it attaches. Assemble the frame (without the glass) and admire!

Note: Once you have the basics of weaving and framing a weaving, you can frame weavings using other skills like LOOPS, RYA, SOUMAK, and KNOTTING (see pages 22–27)!

framed rainbow

~~~~

COLOR STORY

pastel rainbow tones with gold accent

TECHNIQUES

rya knots, lark's head knots

72

rainbow loom

6 yards (6 m) of cotton rug warp

roving in 5 different pastel colors, 1 yard (1 m) of each; I used the Unicorn combed top from Paradise Fibers

scissors

yarn needle

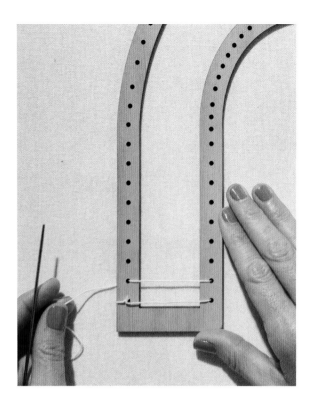 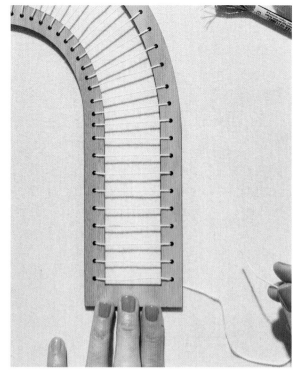

1

Warp up your loom using cotton rug warp. Thread your needle with the cotton rug warp. Pass the needle from the back to the front of the first hole on the bottom left. Hold the yarn at the back and then insert the needle down into the corresponding hole on the right side (inner rim), from the front to the back. Move up to the second hole on the inner rim, and pass the needle from the back to the front and then over to the corresponding hole on the outside rim, and pass it from the front to the back.

2

This is a good time to tie off the starting tail in a double (square) knot.

3

Continue to warp all of the rainbow, moving back and forth until you reach the last hole. Check that the tension is even and springy. Tie a knot with the tail to the warp at the back of the loom.

4

Take your first color of roving and carefully split it down the middle. This gives a thinner, more workable roving. We will weave the outer arc first and move inward to the innermost arc.

5

Using your fingers, weave the roving under the first warp on the left-hand side. Then continue passing over and under each warp until you reach the right-hand side of the rainbow. Be sure to weave loosely. Each time you pass over a warp, the roving should puff out a little bit, undulating over and under the warps with even, loose tension.

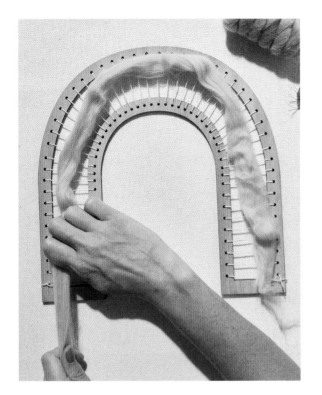
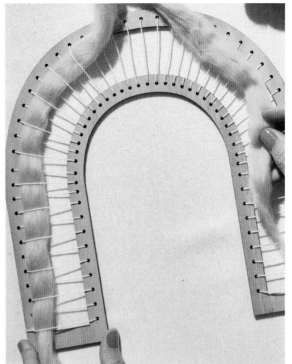
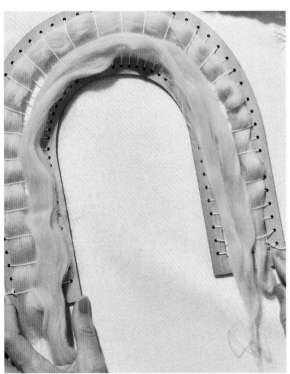
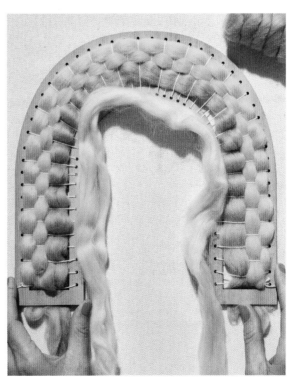

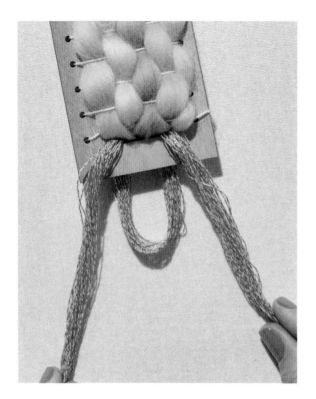

6

Take your second color and repeat. The arc should begin over the first warp on the left-hand side. The arch should continue going under and over the opposite warps to the first arc. Again, be sure to keep the weave loose and even.

7

Continue weaving each arc until you reach the inner edge of the rainbow.

8

We often use rya knots to create fringe, but this type of loom calls for LARK'S HEAD KNOTS (see page 27). I used some thinner gold embroidery thread to create my fringe, about 20 thin strands per knot. Measure the length you want your fringe to be, and then double it and cut. Fold the pieces in half, and pass the loop over the horizontal part of the rainbow. Then pass the tails through the loop. Pull tight. Repeat along the entire horizontal length of both sides (bases) of the rainbow.

woven gift wrap

gift in a box

plain wrapping paper

scissors

yarn needle or shuttle

Scotch tape

yarn in 2 different colors—variegated is particularly eye-catching!

Note: materials for this project are dependent on the size of the gift you are wrapping. Here, I used thick, cotton-like baker's twine, but the weight of the yarn is up to you. Once you have the size of the box you're wrapping, measure the box all the way around and multiply this by ten; this should give you plenty of yarn for the design shown here.

COLOR STORY

analogous color family (blues/purples)

TECHNIQUES

basic tabby

77

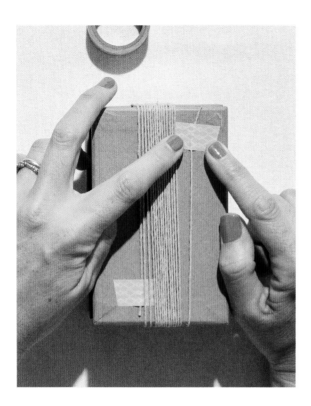
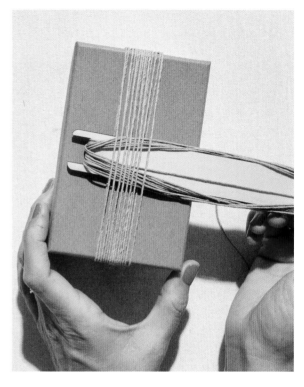

1

Before we begin weaving, you will need to take your gift, put it in a box, and wrap it in plain paper. This will help to create a backdrop to feature your weaving.

2

Take your first color and wrap it once around the longer length of the box. This measurement is the girth, and you will need 10 times this measurement for your warp yarn. Always leave a little extra just in case.

3

Tape one end to the bottom of the box, close to the middle. Begin wrapping the yarn around the box lengthways 10 times, then when you get back to the middle bottom, tape down the end. You have created your warp.

4

Now measure out your other color. Wrap the second color around the box the shorter way. Multiply that girth by 10 and, again leaving a little extra, cut.

5

Take one end of your second color (your weft) and tape it to the bottom of the box. Thread your needle with the other end, or wind it onto a shuttle. Bring the weft up to the top of the box. Once you reach the warp, you will begin to weave a row of BASIC TABBY (see page 20). Pass the weft under the first warp, over the second, and under the third, all the way across until you have woven over and under all of the warp threads.

6

Bring the weft thread around the bottom of the box (there is no need to weave tabby on the bottom of the box) and back up to the top. This time, your row of basic tabby stitches will need to sit on opposite warps. So you will need to go over the first warp, under the second, and over the third. Continue all the way across until you have woven over and under all the warp threads.

7

Continue winding and weaving all the way, until you have created 10 rows of tabby. Then bring the last of the weft around to the bottom and tape down the end.

● intermediate

dovetail coasters

18 × 20-inch (46 × 51 cm) loom

22 yards (20 m) cotton rug warp

55 yards (50 m) bulky-weight yarn (I used Akasha Zeropoint Colorworks Merino)

scissors

yarn needle or shuttle

cardboard

~~~

COLOR STORY

analogous family— pink, orange, rust

TECHNIQUES

twining, lark's head knots, basic tabby, dovetail, batch weaving

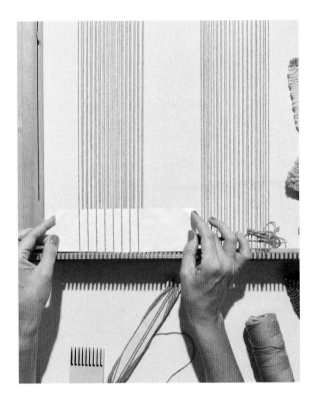

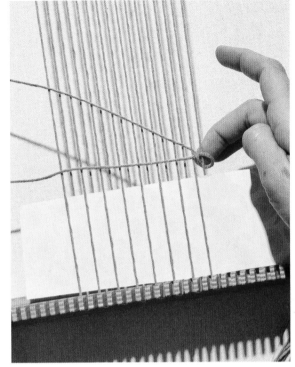

1

Warp up your loom. Tie your cotton rug warp on the top left peg and then draw it down to the bottom-left peg, around, and back up and around the second peg on the top left. Continue along from left to right across your loom until you have warped up 4 inches (10 cm) across. Wrap the warp around the top-right peg, then skip about 1 inch (2.5 cm) and repeat until you have 3 sections warped up, each 4 inches (10 cm) across. Then tie off on the top-right peg.

2

Cut a piece of cardboard about 2 inches (5 cm) high and weave it along the bottom of the weave. This will create a barrier for you to push your weave against and leave space in the warp to tie off and weave back into the coaster.

3

For this project we will create a barrier stitch of TWINING (see page 18). Take 2 yards (2 m) of warp thread and fold it in half. Then create a LARK'S HEAD KNOT (see page 27) by holding the loop over the first warp on the left-hand side. Then pass the tails under the warp and through the loop. Take the tail at the top (tail 1) and pass it under the second warp string. Then take the other tail (tail 2) and pass it above the other tail and then under the third warp string. Pick up 1 and pass it above 2 and under the fourth warp string. Pick up 2 and pass it above 1 and under the fifth warp string. Twine until you get to the end of the row, then tie an overhand or square knot close to the warps. Use the tail of the twining to weave a few rows of BASIC TABBY (see page 20) as a header to the piece. I wove 6 rows of tabby.

4

We will be weaving with two live ends, so load two shuttles or thread two needles with about 2 yards (2 m) each of contrasting colors. If you choose colors that are too similar, the DOVETAIL (see page 30) will not be apparent. One color will be weaving toward the center from the left side, and the other will be weaving toward the center from the right side. The sections will meet roughly in the middle.

5

Take your first color and work basic tabby from the left side toward the middle. Do not weave all the way across. Choose a warp (the DOVETAIL WARP; see page 30) and turn around on that warp and weave back to the left side. Then pick up your second color and weave from the right side to the dovetail warp, and turn around on that warp and weave back to the right side.

6

Pick up your first color on the left and weave back to the dovetail warp, and turn around on that warp and weave back to the left. Then pick up your second color and weave from the right to the dovetail warp, and turn around on that warp and weave back to the right. Note: Both colors are turning around on the same warp. This creates a join between the two colors and a lovely inlay pattern.

7

Continue weaving this dovetail-joined weave for 4 inches (10 cm). We want a square coaster. Pack the wefts tightly together by pushing your weave down against the cardboard. Weave in your ends.

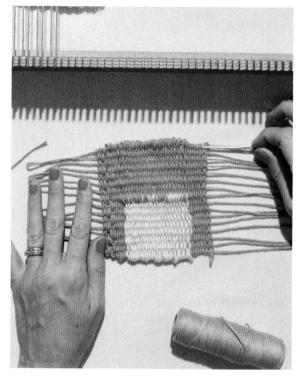

8

Now we need to finish the coaster by creating the border first, and then the barrier of twining using warp thread. Take 2 yards (2 m) of warp and fold the yarn in half. Weave 6 rows of tabby with the warp doubled, and then create a knot around the last warp thread. Don't cut the tails off, but finish with a row of twining, tie a knot, and weave the ends in.

9

You have completed your first coaster. Now move the cardboard spacer to above the completed coaster and BATCH WEAVE (see page 31) two more coasters. Remember you need to give yourself working slack both for the bottom coaster's ends and for the starting ends for the coaster above.

10

Repeat steps 3 to 9 with the remaining warped sections.

11

Now it is time to cut your batch of coasters from the loom. Cut the top and bottom of each coaster, leaving at least 1 inch (2.5 cm) of warp to weave in. Use a needle and weave in each warp thread back vertically into the coaster.

passementerie weaving

18 × 24-inch (45 × 60 cm) loom

15 yards (14 m) cotton rug warp

8 to 10 yards (7.5 to 9 m) each of mid-green bulky-weight wool or thick cord, dark-green bulky-weight wool or thick cord, and peach/pink core-spun bulky-weight wool

scissors

yarn needle or shuttle

weaver's fork (optional)

dowel or rod for hanging

COLOR STORY

complementary colors—green and peach, inspired by flowers in nature

TECHNIQUES

weaving outside the warp, twining, basic tabby, bubble, passementerie, rya

1

Warp up your loom. Tie your cotton rug warp on the top-left peg, then draw it down to the bottom-left peg, around, and back up and around the second peg on the top left. Continue all the way along from left to right across your loom until you reach the last, top-right peg. Wrap the warp thread around the last peg 2 times, but do not tie off yet. You want to check your tension, and you may need to readjust.

2

Check your warp for even and correct tension. It should be springy and even all the way across, and should strum and vibrate when you pass your fingers across the warp threads. If the warp threads stick together, it is too loose. Correct the tension, and when you are happy with it, tie off on the top-right peg. Weave in your weaver's sword and then work in a row of TWINING (see page 18) as a barrier stitch.

3

First you need to prepare your yarns. I chose a mid-green bulky wool. You will need 4 yards (4 m) in length. Thread your needle or load your shuttle. This is your weft. Begin weaving BASIC TABBY (see page 20) at the bottom left across to the right. Check that the knots securing your warp to the loom are at the opposite end from where you start weaving. Basic tabby goes over and under, over and under, all the way across. It doesn't really matter if you begin over or under.

4

Be sure to BUBBLE each row (see page 20) to ensure you are getting even tension all the way up your weave.

5

When you get to the end of your first row, turn back and weave your second row directly above from right to left. This row or pass should be the opposite of the first row. Be sure to bubble. Check that your ends are touching the first and last warps without bagging or pulling in.

6

Continue weaving until the yarn runs out. I wove 14 rows. Weave in your ends by turning back in on the weave; weave the opposite to the row above or below and then vertically back into the color you were just weaving. This will tuck the tail into the weave without its being visible from the front.

7

You have just woven the first tabby section of your piece. We are weaving upside down, from the top of the piece up to the bottom. By doing it this way, we

are left with a nice, neat top to the weaving, with the loops already created using the warp threads.

8

Now we are going to introduce our PASSEMENTERIE (see page 28). Take 2 yards (2 m) of your complementary color. I chose a peach-colored core-spun bulky yarn. Lay this in the opposite shed from the last row of tabby. Leave about 1 inch (2.5 cm) to the beginning of the row on the right side, and the rest will lie to the left, awaiting its turn after the next section of tabby.

9

Now use 4 yards (4 m) of the darker green and weave a second section of tabby, following steps 3 to 7. Make sure that the first row of this section is on the opposite shed to the peach passementerie thread.

13

Take one bunch of 2 lengths and fold them in half like a smile or the letter U. Lay this U across your first 2 warps on the left side of your weave. Pass the left side of the U ends under the first warp thread and back up between the first and the second warp. Then pass the right side of the U ends under the second warp and back up between the first and second warp. Pull up the 4 ends and lay them flat across the top of your rya knot. You have completed your first rya knot. Continue across the weave, tying knots on each pair of warp threads until you have completed the entire row.

14

I created a layered fringe by repeating steps 12 and 13 using longer lengths of green yarn.

15

Finish off your weaving with 3 or 4 rows of tabby to secure your piece. This will sit under the fringe of rya knots, so you can use any yarn you have on hand.

16

Then simply pull the warp loops off the top of your loom and tie some knots in the warp close to the bottom of the weaving, to hold the weaving where you want it to stay. Tying each pair of adjacent warps together works well. Remember that where you just finished weaving is the bottom of the piece, and this part will not be seen.

17

Pop the warp loops off their pegs at the top of the piece (the bottom of the loom); remember that this is the end where you started. As you go, pass a dowel through your loops until all the loops are on the dowel. Be sure to pass it through opposite to the first row of tabby.

10

Once you have woven to the end of the section of tabby, pick up the long length of peach passementerie yarn and lay it in above the section of tabby. Be sure to leave a loop of thread billowing out beyond the last warp thread. This will create an intricate edge.

11

Continue repeating the pattern—tabby/passementerie/tabby—until you are happy with the look. I created 6 blocks of tabby and 5 passes of the passementerie yarn.

12

Now we are going to add a layer of RYA KNOTS (see page 25). My fringe is 7 inches (18 cm) long, which meant that I cut each length at 14 inches (36 cm).

striped weaving

~~~

COLOR STORY

complementary rust/
teal/blue, inspired
by Tasmania's Bay of
Fires

TECHNIQUES

basic tabby, bubble,
rya

12 × 18-inch (30 × 46 cm) loom

15 yards (14 m) cotton rug warp

5 different colors of chunky-
weight yarn in tones of ochre and
blue, 4 yards (3.5 m) of each

200–300 yards (185–275 m)
cotton rug warp in baby blue
for fringe

weaver's sword

scissors

yarn needle or shuttle

12-inch (30 cm) dowel or rod for
hanging

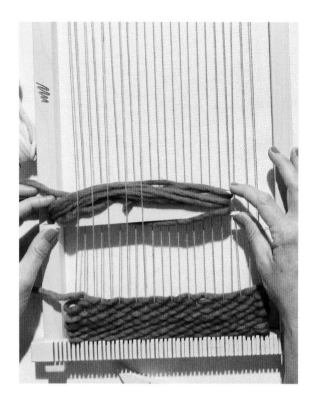

METHOD

1

Warp up your loom. Tie your cotton rug warp on the top-left peg and then draw it down to the bottom-left peg, around, and back up and around the second peg on the top left. Continue all the way along from left to right across your loom until you reach the last, top-right peg. Wrap the warp thread around the last peg 2 times, but do not tie off yet. You want to check your tension, and you may need to readjust.

2

Check your warp for even and correct tension. It should be springy and even all the way across, and should strum and vibrate when you pass your fingers across the warp threads. If the warp threads stick together, it is too loose. Correct the tension, and when you are happy with it, tie off on the top-right peg. Weave in your weaver's sword.

3

Thread your needle or load your shuttle with about 2 yards (2 m) of your first color. This is your weft. Begin weaving BASIC TABBY (see page 20) at the bottom left across to the right. Basic tabby goes over and under, over and under, all the way across. It doesn't really matter if you begin over or under.

4

Be sure to BUBBLE each row (see page 20) to ensure you are getting even tension all the way up your weave. It stops you from pulling too tightly across a pass of tabby.

5

When you get to the end of your first row, turn back and weave your second row directly above, from right to left. This row or pass should be the opposite of the first row. Be sure to bubble. Check that your ends are touching the first and last warps without bagging or pulling in.

6

Continue weaving until the yarn runs out. Weave in your ends by turning back in on the weave; weave the opposite to the row above or below and then vertically back into the color you were just weaving. This will tuck the tail into the weave in the back without its being visible from the front.

7

You have just woven the header of your piece. We are weaving upside down, from the top of the piece up to the bottom. By doing it this way, we are left with a nice, neat top to the weaving, with the loops already created using the warp threads.

8

Now you will begin your stripes! Let's start with vertical stripes. Take 2 yards (2 m) of your first color and 2 yards (2 m) of a contrasting color. Weave one row of color 1. Then weave one row directly above in color 2. Be sure that they are going over the opposite warp threads. Color 1 should finish the row over the last warp, and color 2 should finish under the last warp. Pick up color 1, pass it under color 2, and then over the first warp on the way to create the next row. Pick up color 2; this should pass under the first warp before creating the next row. Now that you are at the over end, you will need to pick up color 1 and pass it over color 2 before passing it under the first warp to create the next row. Pick up color 2 and weave the row, beginning with passing over the first warp. Continue for a few rows until you can see the vertical lines begin to take form.

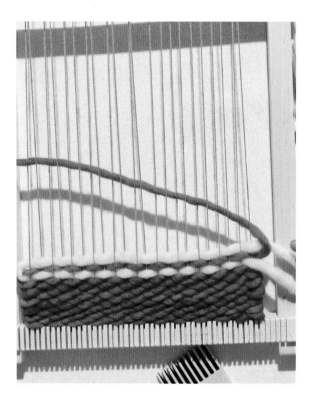

9

It's time to change to horizontal stripes. Weave two rows of color 1, which will bring us back to the same side as color 2. Pick up color 2, pass it under color 1 and then over the first warp before creating two rows in color 2. Pick up color 1 and pass it under color 2, over the first warp, and then weave two rows. Continue weaving until the horizontal lines begin to take form.

10

Create a break by weaving 8 to 10 rows of tabby in color 2.

11

Repeat steps 3 to 10 using color 2 and color 3.

12

Repeat steps 3 to 11 using color 3 and color 4.

13

Repeat steps 3 to 11 using color 4 and color 5.

14

Finish off the pattern with a block of 8 to 10 rows of color 5.

15

Create a layered fringe using RYA KNOTS (see page 25) by first creating a shorter row of thinner-yarn rya knots. My first row of fringe measures one hand-span long once tied, about 4 inches (10 cm). Then lock these in with 16 rows of tabby, using any yarn you have on hand (this will not be seen). Then follow with a layer of fringe that is longer than the first. I chose thicker yarn that will sit two hand-spans (about 8 inches/20 cm) long once tied. Lock in the second row of rya with 3 or 4 rows of tabby.

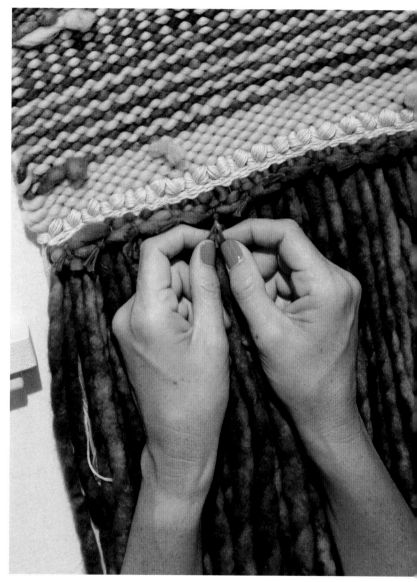

16

To finish, simply cut the warp threads and tie knots in the warp close to the bottom of the weaving (the top of the loom) to hold the weaving where you want it to stay. Knotting each pair of adjacent warp ends works well.

17

One of the most satisfying parts of weaving is hanging your completed piece. Unlike what you did at the top of your weaving (which is the bottom of the piece), you can pop the warp loops off their pegs at the top of the piece (the bottom of the loom). As you go, pass a dowel (or branch, or spoon—experiment!) through your loops until all the loops are on the dowel. Be sure to pass it through opposite to the last row of tabby that you did, over the under warps, and under the over warps. To hang the dowel, tie a piece of yarn to either end. Lift up your weaving and admire your work!

easy

giant off-loom basket weave

~~~

COLOR STORY

analogous color family, blues/greens

TECHNIQUES

lark's head knot, twining, basket weave, piecing, bubble

MATERIALS

clothing rack

18 yards (16 m) each of Echoview Fiber Mill's chunky weight core-spun Merino wool in Kingfisher and Robin's Egg Blue

2 yards (2 m) of cotton cord or string, to tie hanging rod

scissors

1-yard (1 m) dowel or rod for hanging

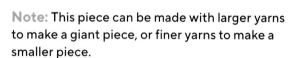

Note: This piece can be made with larger yarns to make a giant piece, or finer yarns to make a smaller piece.

1
Tie your hanging dowel onto a clothing rack at a comfortable height that is higher than the desired length of your piece. If you cannot find a rack at a convenient height, you can use an adjustable-height office chair, or use a succession of different-height chairs or stools.

2
Measure out your yarns for the warp. I measured each piece of core-spun merino at 2 yards (2 m). Cut 23 lengths in color 1 (Kingfisher Teal). These will create our warp.

3
Tie your lengths to the hanging rod, using the LARK'S HEAD KNOT (see page 27). To create a knot, fold the length in half. Place the loop over the rod and pull the tails through the loop. Tighten the knot.

4
Create a row of TWINING (see page 18) where you want the bottom of your weave to be. Keep in mind that unlike in other projects, on this project we are not working upside down, and the bottom really is the bottom. I used the same color as my warp (Kingfisher Teal) to complete the twining. When you get to the end of the row, tie a knot and trim the ends.

7

Then turn back and weave the second row directly above the first, making sure that you are passing over and under the opposite two warps of the row below. Use your fingers to push the row down against the first row. I found that it helped to overcompensate at the selvedges (edges) as I wove, since this style of weave can pull in. By adding a little more weft at the edges, you can create straight vertical edges.

8

Continue weaving rows of basket weave until you run out of weft. Then measure out 6 yards (6 m) of color 2 (Robin's Egg Blue) and double them. Add in new weft by PIECING the yarn (see page 28). To do this, you overlap the 2 ends in opposite directions and pop the tails toward the back. You can weave these tails in vertically once the entire weaving is complete.

9

Continue weaving basket-weave rows up the length of your warp, adding in more weft as you run out. Try to push each row against the row below. If you find that the sides are pulling in, you may need to BUBBLE the weft (see page 20) to maintain consistency.

10

Once you have woven your piece all the way to the top, measure your piece. Check that the sides are even. If they aren't, you may need to pull out a few rows and re-weave at a different spacing and/or tension.

11

Tie off the bottom of the weave in overhand knots of pairs below the row of twining. Leave the outermost warps out of the knots. Trim the fringe to your desired length.

5

Now we will begin the BASKET WEAVE (see page 20). For this project, we take 2 weft threads of the same color and pass them over and then under 2 warp threads. As it is a feature, make sure that the 2 threads do not cross over and do remain in line with each other.

6

Measure out 6 yards (6 m) of color 2 (Robin's Egg Blue), and double it over. Create your first row of basket weave by passing the weft over and under 2 warps at a time all the way across the bottom of your piece. Use your fingers to push the weft close to the row of twining.

macramé tassel

8 yards (7.5 m) of cotton rope or
cord in Mustard, Caramel, Citrine

scissors

~~~

COLOR STORY
**warm-toned
analogous colors**

TECHNIQUE
tassels

103

1

Cut your lengths of rope or cord, determined by how long you want your tassels. You will need 16 lengths. I cut mine to 18 inches (46 cm) each.

2

Divide the lengths into 4 groups of 4 and fold them in half, so that each bunch has a loop at one end.

3

Lay your first bunch horizontally with the loop at the *left* and the tails at the *right*.

4

Pass the loop of your second bunch vertically up through the loop of the first bunch from bottom to top, so that the loop sits above the first bunch.

5

Take the third bunch and pass its loop through the loop of the second bunch, from left to right, and lay it horizontally so that the loop is at the *right* and the tails at the *left*.

6

Pass the loop of the fourth bunch vertically down through the loop of the third bunch from top to bottom, so that the loop sits below the third bunch.

7

Bring the tail from the first bunch through the loop of the fourth bunch.

 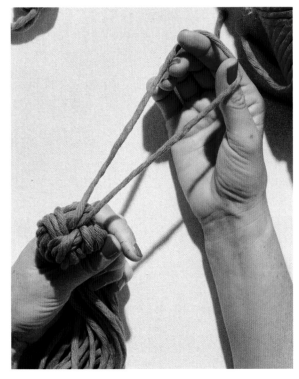

8

Pull the tails carefully to close the knot into a tighter square. Untangle the loops so that the lengths lie neatly next to one another in each section, rather than crossing.

9

Stop once you have a small hole in the middle of the knot. Now we will make a hanger. Take an 18-inch (46 cm) length of the same-color rope or cord and fold it in half. Tie an overhand knot about a hand's width (4 inches/10 cm) down from the loop. Pass this knot into the hole with the loop hanging out the top. The overhand knot should sit inside (under) the macramé knot.

10

If you want a full-skirt (thick) tassel, follow this step. If you want a thinner tassel, skip to step 12. Take another 6 to 8 lengths of rope or cord the same length as the initial pieces (remember we started with 18 inches/46 cm). The more lengths you add at this point, the fuller the tassel skirt will be. Pull the overhand knot from the bottom of the hanger down; this will open a loop inside the larger knot. Pass the new lengths through this loop until the tails are even.

11

Pull the loop of the hanger tight upward; this will draw the new lengths into the original knot. Smooth the lengths down and begin to position the macramé knot sections into place.

12

It's time to secure the tassel lengths by wrapping them together. Take an 18-inch (46 cm) piece of the same rope. Lay the tail vertically along the tassel strands, close to the macramé knot. Hold the end in place with your thumb while you turn the tassel to wrap the rope around the tassel from the top down. Make sure you keep each turn snug to the next one.

13

The last 2 wraps, close to the bottom, should be secured by placing your finger into the wrap and then passing the cord through this loop, twice. This will secure the cord and the bottom of the wrap. Pull tight and trim the end.

14

Trim the end of the tassel and brush out the ends to create a softer look.

107

giant
multi-skirt
tassel

~~~

COLOR STORY
pastel-toned colors

TECHNIQUES
tassel

MATERIALS

very thin yarns or cotton warp in six pastel colors: color 1, 68 yards (62 m); color 2, 67 yards (61 m); color 3, 63 yards (58 m); color 4, 56 yards (51 m); color 5, 46 yards (42 m); color 6, 34 yards (31 m); gold thread for finishing, 1 yard (1 m)

scissors

yarn needle

1

Lay out your yarns in a gradation of pastel colors, one color for each layer. I began with yellow. The first tassel will be the shortest and thickest, and each layer of the tassel will become longer and thinner.

2

Prepare your yarns for your first layer of the tassel. The first one will be 350 lengths of 7 inches (18 cm). Take a 20-inch (50 cm) piece of the same color and tie it around the middle of the bunch with a very tight double (square) knot. This will become the hanger. Allow the tails of the tassel to hang down. Brush out the yarns and trim them neatly.

3

Prepare the yarns for your second layer. This layer will be 300 lengths of 8 inches (20 cm). Take a longer piece of the same color and tie it around the middle of the bunch with a very tight double (square) knot. This will become the hanger that will attach to the first tassel. Allow the tails of the tassel to hang down. Brush out the yarns and trim them neatly. Using the needle, thread the hanging attachment thread of the second tassel through the tie of the first tassel and tie with a double knot.

4

Prepare the yarns for your third layer. This layer will be 250 lengths of 9 inches (23 cm). Take a longer piece of the same color and tie it around the middle of the bunch with a very tight double (square) knot. This will become the hanger that will attach to the inside of the second tassel. Allow the tails of the tassel to hang down. Brush out the yarns and trim them neatly. Using the needle, thread the hanging attachment thread of the third tassel through the tie of the second tassel and tie with a double knot.

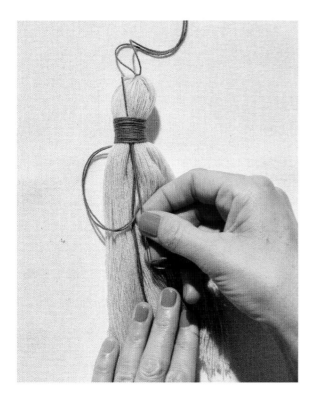 

5

Prepare the yarns for your fourth layer. This layer will be 200 lengths of 10 inches (25 cm). Take a longer piece of the same color and tie it around the middle of the bunch with a very tight double knot. This will become the hanger that will attach to the inside of the third tassel. Allow the tails of the tassel to hang down. Brush out the yarns and trim them neatly. Using the needle, thread the hanging attachment thread of the fourth tassel through the tie of the third tassel and tie with a double knot.

6

Prepare the yarns for your fifth layer. This layer will be 150 lengths of 11 inches (28 cm) long. Take a longer piece of the same color and tie in the middle of the bunch with a very tight double (square) knot. This will become the hanger that will attach to the inside of the fourth tassel. Allow the tails of the

tassel to hang down. Brush out the yarns and trim them neatly. Using the needle, thread the hanging attachment thread of the fifth tassel through the tie of the fourth tassel and tie with a double knot.

7

Prepare the yarns for your sixth layer. This layer will be 100 lengths of 12 inches (31 cm). Take a longer piece of the same color and tie it around the middle of the bunch with a very tight double knot. This will become the hanger that will attach to the inside of the fifth tassel. Allow the tails of the tassel to hang down. Brush out the yarns and trim them neatly. Using the needle, thread the hanging attachment thread of the sixth tassel through the tie of the fifth tassel and tie with a double knot.

8

Pick up the hanging threads from the first tassel and allow all the tassels to fall over one another. Give the whole lot a big shake, and use your hands to arrange the tassel layers into place.

9

Now we can wrap the top tassel to finish it off. Take 1 yard (1 m) of the first tassel's yarn and lay the end along the top of the top tassel. Hold it in place with your thumb, and begin to wrap the thread around the top of the tassel. Make sure that each turn is below but snug to the layer above. Continue to wrap until you have wrapped about 10 times. Use a needle to thread the end of the wrapper into itself, and trim the ends.

10

Tie an overhand knot in the hanging thread and make one final trim.

framed circular weaving

9-inch (23 cm) circular loom

6 yards (5.5 m) cotton rug warp

1 yard (1 m) each of Roving Textiles Extra Fine Merino Wool Roving in Twilight, Fog, Honey, Milk; 2 yards (2 m) of Handpainted Ribbon in Sunrise; 2 yards (2 m) of thick yarn in Hedwig; 2 yards (2 m) of thinner yarn in Stardust

scissors

yarn needle

~~~~

COLOR STORY

complementary colors— mustard and lilac

TECHNIQUES

basic tabby, bubble, soumak, knots, loops

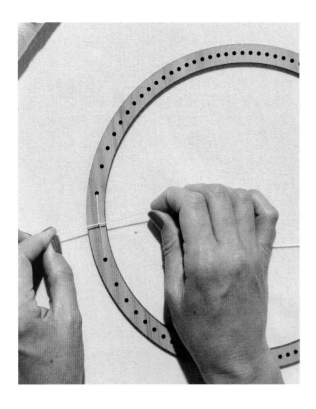

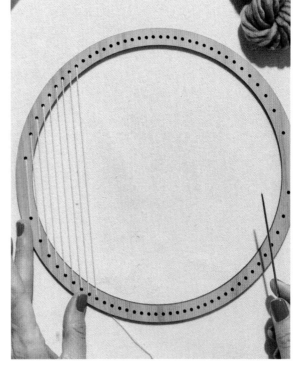

METHOD

1

Warp up your loom using cotton rug warp. Thread your needle with about 6 yards (6 m) of cotton rug warp. Pass it from the back to the front of the first hole on the bottom left (nine o'clock position). Hold the thread at the back and then bring the needle over to the corresponding hole on the top side. Pass it from the front to the back. Move along to the next hole up, and pass the warp from the back to the front and then down to the corresponding hole, and pass it from the front to the back.

2

This is a good time to tie off the tail in a double knot.

3

Then continue to warp all of the circle, moving up and down and front to back until you reach the last hole on the right side. Check that the tension is even and springy. Tie a knot with the tail to the warp at the back of the loom.

4

For this design we will use a background of creamy white tones and leave the colors for the accents. The shapes we create will be organic and fluid.

5

Begin at the bottom left of the circle. Weave a few rows of BASIC TABBY (see page 20), over and under. I made my shape get smaller as I wove each row. Be sure to BUBBLE on each pass (see page 20) to ensure you are not pulling too tight. Weave the tails back into the weaving from the back as you finish each shape.

6

I chose a few different shades and weights of cream to create the creamy white part of the design. Weave some organic shapes. These shapes do not interlock but sit flush against one another. Fill in about a third of the circle.

7

Once you are happy with your base, you can change to the colored section. Use a mixture of SOUMAK, basic tabby, KNOTS, and LOOPS (see pages 20–26). Be sure to lock in the stitches by weaving in the tails in the back.

8

Once you have filled in the second third of the area, it's time to fill the rest with organic tabby shapes in creamy white. Weave in the tails from the back.

macramé
feather earrings

¼ inch (5 mm) single-ply cotton cord or string

sharp scissors or rotary cutter

cutting mat

macramé brush or pet brush

ruler or measuring tape

fixing or stiffening spray

hook earring findings

~~~~~

COLOR STORY
gold
TECHNIQUES
macramé knotting

117

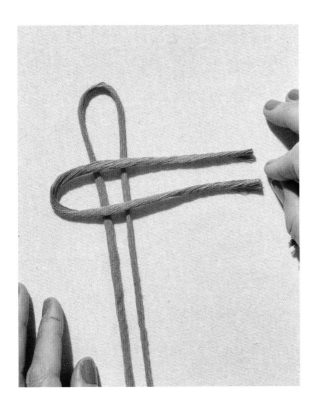

Note: This project is so fun and versatile. You can use the same basic tutorial to create feathers, leaves, rainbows, or even hearts, depending on how you trim and shape the final piece.

1

Measure out and cut the lengths of your cord:
- 1 × 12 inches (30 cm) for the spine of the feather.
- 10 × 8 inches (20 cm) for the horizontal lengths (you can choose one or a variety of colors)

2

Take the spine strip and fold it in half, with the loop at the top. This will create the loop to hang the final feather from, and the spine on which to tie the knots.

3

Take 2 of the horizontal lengths. We will be working in pairs to create each knot. Fold each piece in half. Place one loop under the spine of the feather, with the tails pointing right. Take the second piece and lay it over the top of the spine of the feather, with the tails pointing left. Take the tails of the top piece and pass them through the loop of the bottom piece, and pass the tails of the bottom piece up through the loop of the top piece. Pull tight. This is the knot you will be using to create your whole feather.

4

We want to see the spine of the feather to create a pattern of alternating knots, so the second knot needs to be created in the opposite direction. Fold two horizontal pieces in half. Place the first looped piece under the spine of the feather, with the tails pointing *left* this time. Then take your second piece and lay it over the top of the spine, with the tails pointing *right*. Take the tails of the top piece and pass them through the loop of the bottom piece, and pass the tails of the bottom piece up through the loop of the top piece. Pull tight.

119

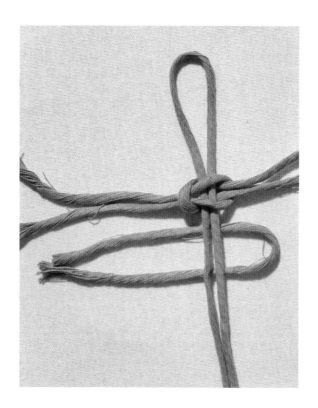

5

Continue working your way through the cords until you have completed the knots. As you finish each knot, you can snug it up by holding the middle length of spine and pushing the knot up. Be sure not to push too far over the hanging loop!

6

Now you will give it a little haircut. Lay the piece down on a cutting mat or a piece of cardboard. Pull the rope knots into place. You can create a little paper template or be confident and cut freehand. This will not be the final cut, just more of a general shape.

7

Time for a brush—this is the most satisfying part. Take a macramé brush or pet brush and begin brushing out the strands on each side. Hold the knots at the spine and brush from the spine out. You will need to brush hard, and each section will need a few passes. Begin at the top of the feather and work your way down.

8

Read the instructions on the stiffening spray before using. Follow the instructions and give your whole feather 2 to 3 layers of spray, being sure to wait for each layer to dry before applying another layer.

9
You will notice the edges of your feather are uneven and will need to give them one final trim. Be sure to use very sharp scissors or a rotary cutter. Cut a little at a time, so you can control how the shape is forming.

10
Give your feather one last coat of stiffening spray and let dry.

11
Take some matching cotton thread and tie a knot through the loop of your earring hook. Attach it to the top of the macramé loop.

121

looped woven necklace

12 × 16-inch (30 × 40 cm) piece of thick cardboard

thick cotton in a variety of colors but similar thicknesses, 18 yards (16.5 m) each (or finer yarn/ floss with multiple strands held together, 72 yards/66 m total)

scissors

needle or shuttle

weaver's fork

COLOR STORY
analogous cool tones

TECHNIQUES
basic tabby, bubble, twining

METHOD

1

Choose the color you want to have as the length of your necklace; this is your warp. I used a thick bamboo-cotton blend. Hold or tape the end to the back of the loom or cardboard near the top, then wrap it around the longer part of the cardboard 20 times. The warp will go around both sides of the card, and we will weave on both sides.

2

Check your warp for even and correct tension. It should be springy and even all the way across, and should strum and vibrate when you pass your fingers across the warp threads. If the warp threads stick together, it is too loose. Correct the tension, and when you are happy with it, tie off the end to the beginning by tying in a simple double (square) knot.

3

For the weft sections I chose embroidery floss. It comes in a variety of colors in small amounts. I wanted the yarns to be the same thickness, so I folded the embroidery thread over 4 times to create a thicker ply. Two yarns of similar thicknesses (the warp and the weft) woven together will create a checkerboard effect, and that is what we are going for. Thread your needle with the quadrupled floss; this is your weft. Begin weaving BASIC TABBY (see page 20) at the bottom left across to the right. Basic tabby goes over and under, over and under, all the way across. It doesn't really matter if you begin over or under.

4

Be sure to BUBBLE each row (see page 20) to ensure you are getting even tension all the way up your weave. Cotton can be especially toothy or grippy, so it is extra important to bubble the weft, or the weave will end up drawing in.

5

When you get to the end of your first row, turn back and weave your second row directly above, from right to left. This row or pass should be the opposite of the first row. Be sure to bubble, and push the weft into place with a weaver's fork. Check that your ends are touching the first and last warps without bagging or pulling in.

6

Continue weaving until the yarn runs out. Weave the ends in by turning back in on the weave, and pass along the edge. This will add a border effect.

7

Repeat steps 3 to 6 with a different color.

8

Repeat steps 3 to 6 with the original color. This will create a color-block pattern.

9

Lock in the basic tabby stitches at the top and bottom of this section by working 2 rows of TWINING (see page 18) as follows: Take a length of yarn at least 12 times the width of the necklace. Fold it in half, and begin twining over the first 2 warps on the left-hand side. Note: This is different from the single-warp-thread twining we have done before, since we are working with warp pairs this time. Pass the top piece under the second set of warps. Then pass the original piece under the third set of warps and then the other piece under the fourth set of warps. Work all the way across. When you get to the end, turn around and twine a second row.

10

Repeat steps 3 to 9 on the opposite side of the cardboard loom.

11

Slip the necklace off the loom and add it to your favorite outfit!

127

wrapped keychain

~~~~~

COLOR STORY
pastel rainbow

TECHNIQUES
fiber sculpture, wrapping

three 12-inch (30 cm) pieces of natural-colored rope or cord

cotton embroidery floss in four pastel shades, 3 yards (2.5 m) each; and in metallic gold, 2 yards (2 m)

sharp scissors

sewing needle and thread in a neutral shade

macramé brush or pet brush

split-ring keychain attachment

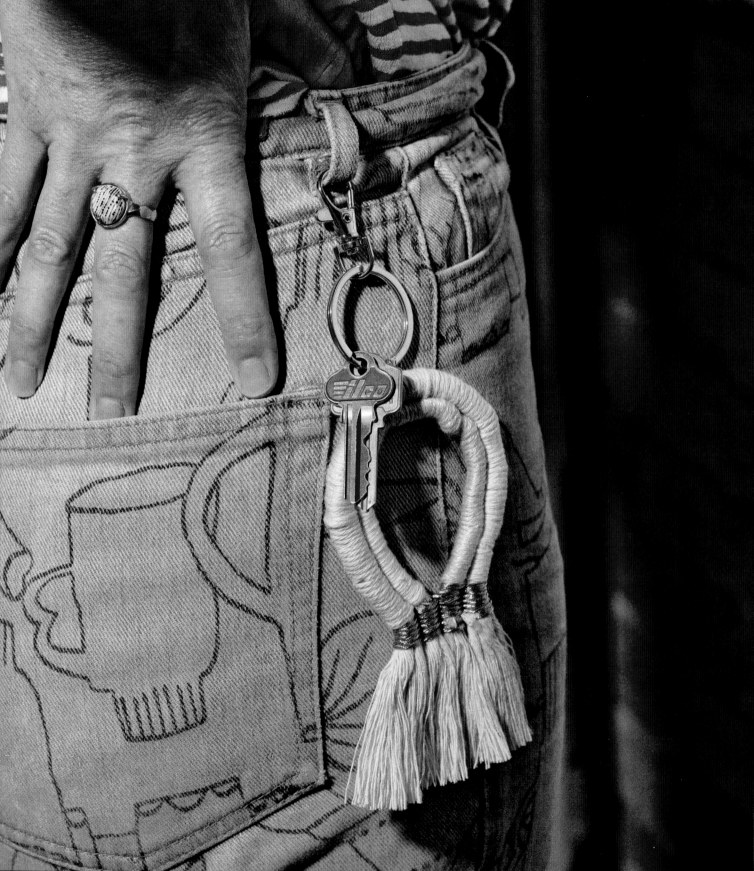

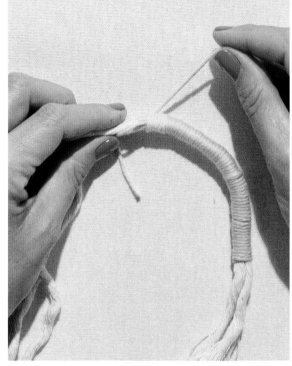

METHOD

1

First form the outside layer of the rainbow. Cut 3 strips of rope or cord to about half the length of your arm.

2

Take your first color of pastel cotton floss and lay its tail on the ropes, pointing away from the end of the ropes, and about 1 inch (2.5 cm) from the end. Hold it in your hand, with your thumb holding the floss tail in place. Begin to wrap around the ropes, back down over the tail of the floss. Be sure not to cross over any wrap and that each one sits flush and snug with the next wrap. The wraps should be firm and neat without being too tight. I find it easiest to hold the bundle in my non-dominant hand and wrap with my dominant hand.

3

Keep wrapping and gently shaping as you wrap to form a curve.

4

If you want to change color, snip off the first color with about 1 inch (2.5 cm) of tail. Lay the tail along the length of the ropes, then lay the tail of the new color alongside it, and continue wrapping.

5

Once you have wrapped a curved rainbow shape, leave a tail of at least 2 inches (5 cm), securing the last turn by passing the end under the previous wrap. Set this section aside.

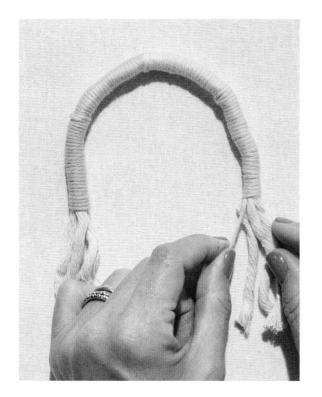

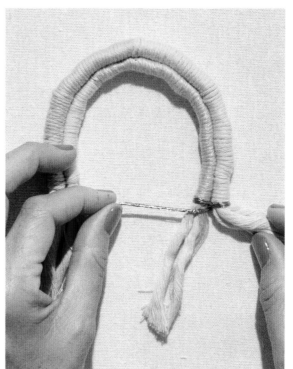

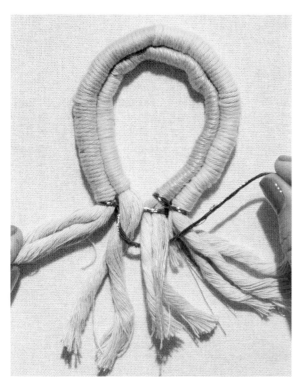

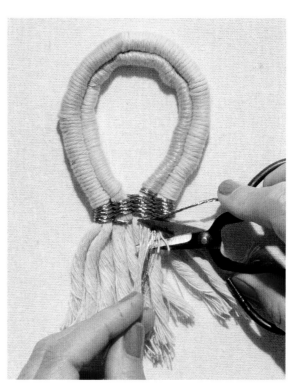

131

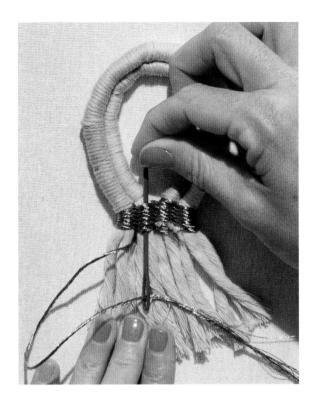 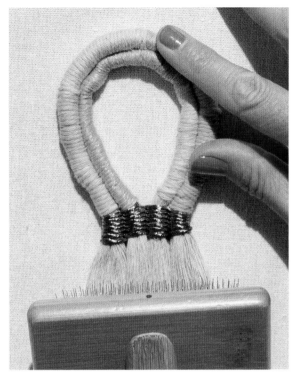

6
Using 2 strips of rope to create the inner layer, repeat steps 1 to 4. Keep checking that the curve will fit nicely into the outer layer; this one is a tighter bend.

7
Place the smaller curve inside the larger curve. Take your needle and thread and sew the two curves together.

8
Now you'll bind the ends together using a figure-8 pattern. I used metallic gold embroidery floss. Then use the needle to tuck the end back into the wrapping.

9
Trim any colored threads, and brush out the tails using a macramé brush or pet brush. Give the tails one last trim with very sharp scissors.

10
Use some of your embroidery floss to sew the weaving onto a keychain attachment.

133

wrapped rainbow cake topper

~~~

COLOR STORY
bright rainbow

TECHNIQUES
fiber sculpture, wrapping

MATERIALS

cotton rope or cord in 5 different bright colors, 20 inches (50 cm) each

variety of cotton embroidery floss in 5 bright shades to match and 1 metallic thread, 1 yard (1 m) of each

sharp scissors, or rotary cutter

sewing needle and thread in a neutral shade

macramé brush or pet brush

2 wooden skewers

METHOD

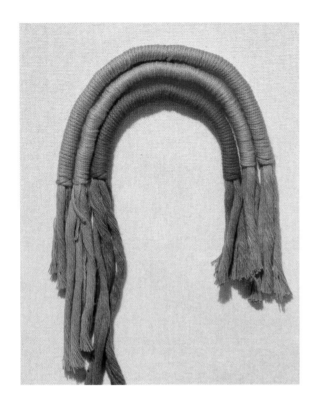
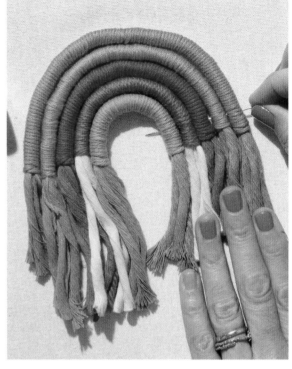

1
This rainbow will have 5 layers. First we will form the outside layer of the rainbow. Cut one color of rope or cord to about half the length of your arm, and hold it lengthwise.

2
Take your first color of bright cotton floss and lay the tail in the opposite direction to the tail of the rope, about 2 inches (5 cm) from the end of the rope. You will start wrapping at that point, so that some of the rope is left unwrapped. Hold it all in your hand, with your thumb holding the cotton tail in place. Begin to wrap around the rope, back along over the tail of the cotton floss. Be sure not to cross over any wrap and that each sits flush with the next wrap. The wraps should be firm and neat without being too tight. I find it easiest to hold the bundle in my non-dominant hand and wrap with my dominant hand.

3
Keep wrapping and gently shaping with your hands to form a curve.

4
If you want to change color, snip off the first color with about 1 inch (2.5 cm) of tail. Lay the tail of the wrap with the rope, then lay the tail of the new color along with it. Then continue wrapping.

5
Once you have wrapped a curved rainbow shape, leave a tail of the inside cord of at least 2 inches (5 cm). Secure the wrap and set this section aside.

6
Cut strips of rope to create the inner layers, and repeat steps 1 to 4 with each successive color. Keep checking that the curves will fit nicely into the layer outside each inner layer.

7
Place the smaller curves inside the larger curves. Take your needle and thread and sew the curves together.

8
Bind each of the ends together using a figure-8 pattern. I used metallic gold embroidery thread. Then use the needle to tuck the end back into the wrapping.

9
Trim any colored threads and brush out the tails of the cord using a pet brush or macrame brush. Give the tails one last trim with very sharp scissors or a rotary cutter.

10
Slip the wooden skewers up into the wrapping with the pointy end aimed down.

● advan
ced

magic no-sew cushion

MATERIALS

cardboard loom equal to the size you want your cushion to be; I used 18 × 20 inches (46 × 51 cm)

Scotch tape

cotton rug warp

82 yards (75 m) super-chunky yarn; I used Roving Textiles Superfluff in Kaleidoscope

scissors

yarn needle or shuttle

ruler

fiberfill

COLOR STORY
rainbow jewel tones

TECHNIQUES
bubble, piecing, loops, basic tabby, tassels

139

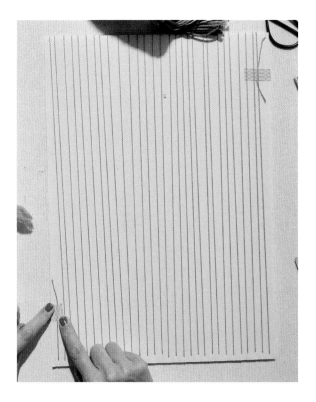
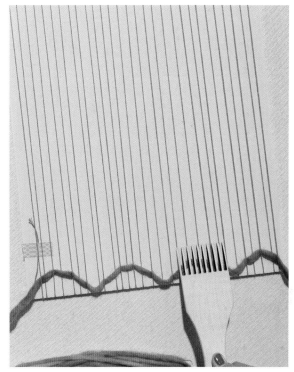

1

Before beginning to weave, you'll need to set up your loom by attaching your warp. For this project, we'll be weaving around the loom in a horizontal spiral, creating a two-layer fabric on the front and back of the loom. Begin by measuring and cutting notches in your cardboard, about 3 notches per 1 inch (2.5 cm), on the top and bottom of your cardboard loom. Next, slide the end of your warp into the first notch at the top (tape it down), and start vertically wrapping the warp down to and around the bottom of your loom, using the notches at the bottom to maintain alignment, and back up the other side. When you hit a top notch, also wrap the warp around the peg (in one notch, over and out the next notch over), and pass the warp back down on that side of the loom. This will make your warp threads align correctly, and will ensure there is an opening. The loops will overlap at the top, and each notch will hold 2 warp threads, but that won't be an issue. Warp your loom completely, making sure you have an odd number of warp strings. Note: the last warp ends at the bottom; secure it after it goes through the notch with a bit of tape. That way, you can continuously weave around the loom in a spiral. This way of warping will create a pocket with the top open and the bottom and sides woven together.

2

To start weaving, thread your needle with 1 yard
(1 m) of yarn. Begin at the bottom left of the loom
by weaving under the first warp thread and over
the second. Continue going along, under and over,
until you've finished the row on the front of your
loom, leaving a 2-inch (5 cm) tail hanging where
you started. Remember to BUBBLE your weft (see
page 20), as always, and push your weft into place
with the weaver's fork. Continue on past the edge
of your loom, around the corner and weaving on the
back side of your loom. Keep weaving upward in a
spiral, going around the entire loom, until you've
reached your desired height or need to begin with a
new piece of yarn. You can either tie on a new piece
or try PIECING the yarn (see page 28) by laying the
tails over each other and poking them toward the
cardboard.

143

3

To add some texture to my pillow, I decided to add LOOPS (see page 22) in the middle.

4

After adding texture, finish the pillow with BASIC TABBY (see page 20), going all the way to the top. When you're ready to take your piece off the loom, pop your loops of warp threads off the cardboard loom at the top. Slide the loom out of the middle of your pillow, bending the cardboard if you need to.

5

Fill the pocket with fiberfill and tie the end loops to one another. If you have managed to weave clear to the top and you don't have enough room to tie, you can sew or crochet the loops to one another to close the end.

6

To add more texture and a decorative flair, you can attach TASSELS to the corners of your pillow (see page 30) using your desired yarn. Use the string you first tied in the middle of the tassel to attach each piece to its own corner. Finally, trim any stray pieces and decide where your new accent cushion will live!

embroidered laptop sleeve

cardboard loom: measure your laptop or device the sleeve is for and create a loom approximately 1 inch (2.5 cm) wider and longer

40 yards (37 m) of super-chunky yarn in color 1, and 3–4 yards (3–4 m) in color 2; I used Roving Textiles Superfluff in Peace and Mojave Ruse

scissors

needle or shuttle

Scotch tape

ruler

cotton rug warp

COLOR STORY

complementary colors—blue and rust

TECHNIQUES

couching, bubble, piecing

145

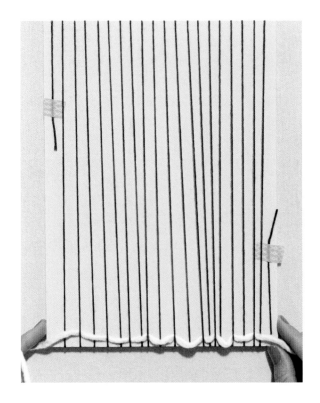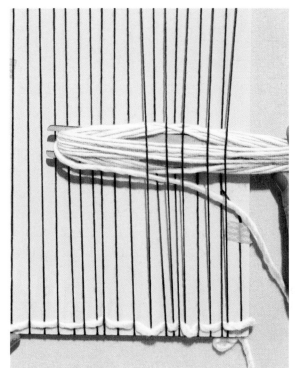

METHOD

Note: In embroidery, couching and laid work are techniques in which yarn or other materials are laid across the surface of the ground fabric and fastened in place with small stitches of the same or a different yarn.

1

Before beginning to weave, you'll need to set up your loom by attaching your warp string. For this project, we'll be weaving around the loom in a spiral, creating fabric on the front and back of the loom. Begin by measuring and cutting notches in your cardboard, about 3 notches per 1 inch (2.5 cm), on the top and bottom of your loom. Then slide the end of your warp into the first notch at the top (secure it with tape) and start vertically wrapping the warp down and around the bottom of your loom and back up the other side, using the bottom notches for alignment. When you hit a top notch, also wrap the warp horizontally around the "peg" (in one notch,

over and out the next notch over) and pass the warp back down on that same side you just came up. This will make your warp threads align correctly. It will also mean there are 2 warp yarns in each notch, and overlapping loops, but that is correct. Warp your loom completely, making sure that you have an odd number of warp strings. Note: the last warp ends at the bottom; secure it after it goes through the notch with a bit of tape. That way, you can continuously weave around the loom in a spiral. This way of warping will create a pocket with the top open and the bottom and sides woven together.

2

To start weaving, thread your shuttle with 1 yard (1 m) of yarn. Begin at the bottom of the loom by weaving under the first warp thread and over the second. Continue going along under and over, BUBBLING the weft (see page 20) and pushing it into place with the weaver's fork, until you've finished the row on the

147

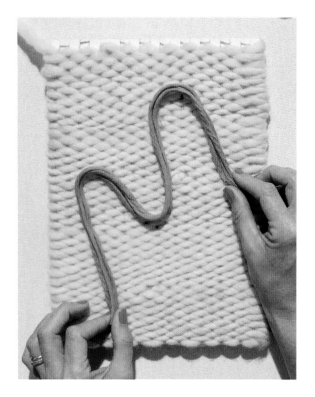 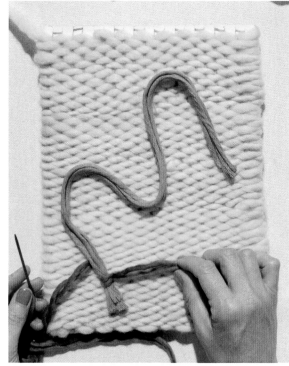

front of your loom, leaving a 2-inch (5 cm) tail hanging where you started. Continue on past the edge of your loom, turning to the other side, and weave on the back side of your loom. Keep weaving upward in a spiral, going around the entire loom, until you've reached your desired height or need to begin with a new piece of yarn. You can either tie on a new piece or try PIECING the yarn (see page 28) by laying the tails over each other and poking them toward the back.

3
Continue to weave all the way up the loom in a circle until you reach the top. This will create a pocket with an open top.

4
Use some paper to work out your couching design, or simply play with the yarn to lay out your design. I made an abstract design on one side and my initials on the other side.

5
Choose a color for the couching that complements the design color, and thread your needle. Begin stitching (couching) your design onto your woven background. Push your tails toward the back using a needle. This is much easier with the cardboard still in place!

6
When you're ready to take your piece off the loom, pop your loops of warp threads off the cardboard loom at the top. Slide the loom out of the middle of your sleeve, bending the cardboard if you need to. Then weave the 2 tail ends of your warp vertically back into your piece, using a tapestry needle. This will secure your ends and hide the warp.

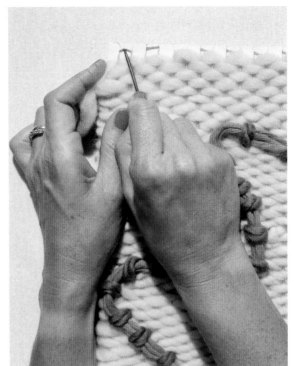

off-loom statement

MATERIALS

~~~

COLOR STORY
monotone—rust,
terra-cotta, natural

TECHNIQUES
macra-weave,
lark's head knot

clothing rack

chunky-weight core-spun yarn;
I used Echoview Fiber Mill in the
colors Cedar Waxing, 24 yards
(22 m); Redwing, 12 yards (11 m);
and Hedwig, 45 yards (41 m)

cotton cord or string to tie
hanging rod

scissors

24-inch (60 cm) dowel or rod for
hanging

Note: The fundamental idea behind macra-weave (like, macrame) is tracking the live ends as they change from warp to weft and back to warp again.

1

Tie your hanging rod onto a clothing rack at a comfortable height that is higher than the desired length of your piece.

2

Measure out your yarns. I measured each piece 3 yards (3 m) long—15 lengths of Hedwig, 8 lengths of Cedar Waxing, 4 lengths of Redwing.

3

Tie your lengths to the hanging rod using the LARK'S HEAD KNOT (see page 27). To create a knot, fold the length in half. Place the loop over the rod and pull the tails through the loop. Pull tight. We are going to use these lengths as warp.

4

I created a pattern with my lengths: 3 Hedwig, 1 Cedar Waxing, 1 Redwing, 1 Cedar Waxwing. Repeat across the length of rod, 4 total repeats, ending with 3 Hedwig to balance.

5

Find the middle pair (it should be in Hedwig if you have chosen the same pattern as mine). Take the right leg of the pair—we will call this the "live end"— and weave it across the hanging warps to the left, under one, and over one.

6

Then take the left leg of the next pair to the right of the middle; this is the next strand to the right. Weave this live end across the hanging warps to the left. Be sure to weave opposite to the row above.

7

Take the next strand to the right and weave as a live end across the hanging warps to the left. Continue until you have woven all the strands on the right side of the rod, using all of the pieces and weaving them over to the left.

8

Push these wefts up toward the hanging rod, so that each weft sits at a diagonal and pulls the warp threads into the opposite diagonal direction.

9

Split the ends into two halves, left and right. I draped them behind and over a little hook at the sides of the clothing rack, or simply tie them back. The important part is just to keep track of where the middle is.

10

Take the uppermost piece from the left side (live piece/weft) and weave it over and under each hanging piece on the left side (warps) until you reach the middle, and pass it over or under the middle-most piece from the right side (work one strand past the middle).

153

11

Now take the uppermost piece from the right side (live piece/weft) and weave it over and under each hanging piece on the right side (warps) until you reach the middle, and pass it over or under the middle-most piece from the left side (again, just one strand past the middle).

12

Repeat steps 10 and 11, continuing to work the outermost/uppermost piece from each side, alternating with the outermost piece from the other side, back to one strand past the middle, until the color order of the hanging yarns returns to the original order and you have woven each of the side pieces back into the middle. As you are weaving, continue to move the wefts up and evenly into place.

13

To finish, take each pair of matching pieces and tie an overhand knot.

trapped rya weaving

COLOR STORY

analogous color gradation

TECHNIQUES

basic tabby, bubble, rya

MATERIALS

20 × 35-inch (50 × 90 cm) loom

chunky-weight yarn; I used core-spun Echoview Fiber Mill Rug Yarn in Hedwig, 22 yards (20 m)

2 yards (2 m) each We Are Knitters The Wool (100% wool; 87 yards [80 m] per 7-ounce [200 g] ball) in Navy Blue, Denim Blue, Sky Blue, Aquamarine, and Forest Green

2 yards (2 m) each Roving Textiles Jungle Yarn (50% Bluefaced Leicester wool, 50% Merino wool; 110 yards [100 m] per 4½-ounce [125 g] skein) and Roving Textiles Superfluff (100% Merino wool; 82 yards [75 m] per 4½-ounce [125 g] skein)

22 yards (20 m)

³⁄₁₆-inch (4 mm) of cotton rug warp

scissors

shuttle

weaver's fork (optional)

24-inch (60 cm) dowel or rod for hanging

 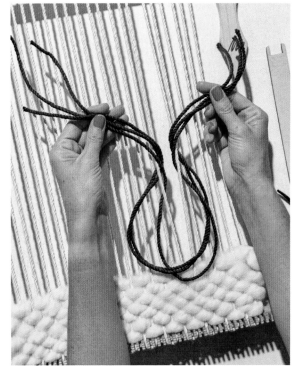

1

Warp up your loom with cotton rug warp. I used 3/16-inch (4 mm) cotton cord. This will give a chunkier look to the final piece, and the cotton cord will create the fringe. Tie your cotton rug warp on the top-left peg and then draw it down to the bottom-left peg, around, and back up and around the second peg on the top left. Continue all the way along from left to right across your loom until you reach the last, top-right peg. Wrap the warp thread around the last peg 2 times, but do not tie off yet. You want to check your tension, and you may need to readjust.

2

Check your warp for even and correct tension. It should be springy and even all the way across, and should strum and vibrate when you pass your fingers across the warp threads. If the warp threads stick together, it is too loose. Correct the tension, and when you are happy with it, tie off on the top-right peg.

3

I chose to create the header of my piece using chunky core-spun yarn from Echoview Fiber Mill. Measure out and cut 4 yards (4 m) in length. Load your shuttle with the yarn. This is the weft. Begin weaving BASIC TABBY (see page 20) at the bottom left, across to the right. Check that the knots connecting your warp to the loom are at the opposite end of the weaving from where you are starting. Basic tabby goes over and under, over and under, all the way across. It doesn't really matter if you begin over or under.

4

Be sure to BUBBLE each row (see page 20) to ensure you are getting even tension all the way up your weave.

157

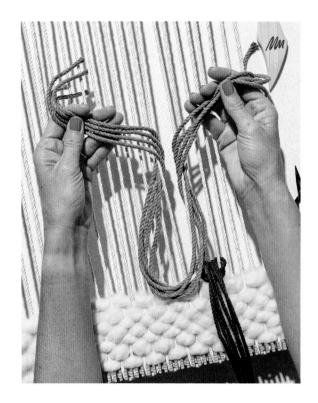

5

When you get to the end of your first row, turn back and weave your second row directly above, from right to left. This row or pass should be the opposite of the first row. Be sure to bubble. Check that your ends are touching the first and last warps without bagging or pulling in.

6

Continue weaving until the yarn runs out. I wove 8 rows. Weave in your ends by turning back in on the weave; weave the opposite to the row above or below and then vertically back into the color you were just weaving. This will tuck the tail into the weave without its being visible from the front.

7

You have just woven the first tabby section of your piece. We are weaving upside down, from the top of the piece up to the bottom. By doing it this way, we are left with a nice, neat top to the weaving, with the loops already created using the warp threads.

8

Now we will begin the trapped RYA color gradation (see page 25). I have chosen a variety of blues and greens from We Are Knitters and Roving Textiles. Prepare your yarns—use 3 to 4 yards (3 to 4 m) of each color in each rya knot, and fold it over; we'll ultimately work with tails that have 4 strands. Fold this in half again to create the loop for the rya knot. Tie a row of rya knots across (I began with Navy Blue, Denim Blue, Sky Blue, Aquamarine, Jungle Yarn, Superfluff, Forest Green). Leave a few inches at either side that will create a white border, once we fill in the rest of the weaving.

9

Now we will lock in the rya knots using chunky yarn (I used core-spun). Weave 4 rows of basic tabby all the way across the piece below the rya knots (remember we are weaving upside down). Lay the tails of the rya knots over these rows of tabby, then lock them down using a row of tabby. Then lift them up and weave 4 more rows of tabby. Repeat this process of trapping on 1 row of tabby and then locking in with 4 rows of tabby. I repeated the process 7 more times.

10

Finish off your weaving with 3 or 4 rows of tabby to secure your piece.

11

Then simply pull the warp loops off your loom and tie some knots in the warp close to the bottom of the weaving, to hold the weaving where you want it to stay. Overhand knots work well here, or you can cut the loops and tie adjacent pairs of warps together. This all becomes fringe.

12

One of the most satisfying parts of weaving is hanging your completed piece. Like what you (maybe) did at the bottom of your weaving, you can pop the warp loops off their pegs at the top (remember that we wove upside down). As you go, pass a rod (or branch, or spoon—experiment!) through your loops until all the loops are on the rod. Be sure to pass the rod through opposite to the last row of tabby that you did. To hang the rod, tie a piece of yarn to each end. Lift up your weaving and admire your work!

159

twill
heat mat

~~~

COLOR STORY
warm-toned monotone

TECHNIQUES
twining, twill

12 × 18-inch (30 × 46 cm) loom

5 yards (5 m) cotton cord to be used as weft; I used Recycled Luxe Macrame Rope from Mary Maker Studio, in Terracotta

orange cotton rug warp

scissors

yarn needle or shuttle

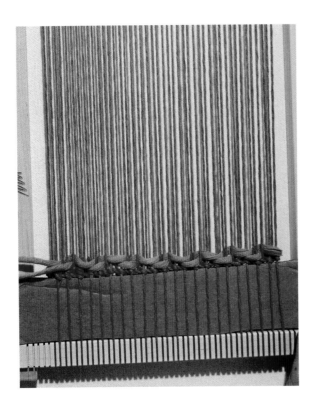

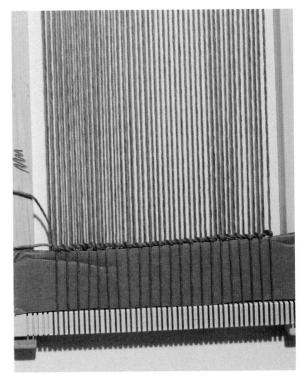

1

Warp up your loom. Tie your orange cotton rug warp on the top-left peg and then draw it down to the bottom-left peg, around, and back up and around the second peg on the top left. Continue all the way along from left to right across your loom until you reach about 8 inches (20 cm) across, stopping at the top-right peg. Wrap the warp thread around the last peg 2 times, but do not tie off yet. You want to check your tension, and you may need to readjust.

2

Check your warp for even and correct tension. It should be springy and even all the way across, and should strum and vibrate when you pass your fingers across the warp threads. If the warp threads stick together, it is too loose. Correct the tension, and when you are happy with it, tie off on the top-right peg.

3

This project will function as a mat, so there will be no top or bottom. We will begin and finish the project with a row of TWINING (see page 18). Take 2 yards (2 m) of the orange warp thread and fold it in half. Measure about 3 inches (7 cm) from the bottom of the loom, and pass one end behind the first warp on the left side. Then take the other end and pass it behind the second warp thread to the right. Then take the first end and pass it behind the third warp thread and continue along until you have twined all the way across. Tie an overhand knot to hold the twining in place.

4

We will be weaving TWILL (see page 30) in this project. Once you have worked out how many warps you have, you can draw this pattern out. If you have any experience with weaving, you will know that woven fabric needs to create tension between rows

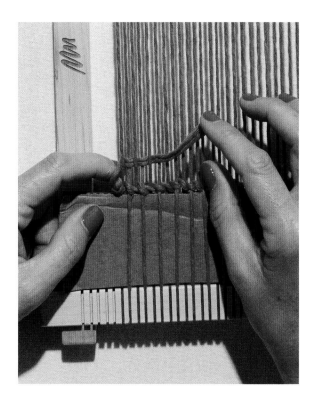

to achieve the tension needed to hold itself together. If you look at the ends of this pattern, you will see there are 5 rows that all finish under the warps. This will not work, so we need to color in to represent one over and one under in a pattern, to create the correct pattern to hold the piece together.

5

Thread your needle or load your shuttle with about 2 yards (2 m) of cotton cord. Look at the pattern pictured here to help you visualize. The colored squares are over, and the uncolored squares pass under the warp threads. Begin on the left side and move across to the right side of the project. Pass over the first 3 warps and then under the second 3 warps, over the next 3 warps and under the next 3, until you get to the end of your first row. You will finish under the last warp.

6

When you get to the end of your first row, turn back and weave your second row directly above, from right to left. Follow the pattern. You will begin over the first warp.

7

Continue weaving until the yarn runs out. For this project I loaded my shuttle or threaded my needle with another 2 yards (2 m) and simply tied on the new end to the end in the project. I wove this pattern for 10 inches (25 cm) before tucking the ends into the back.

8

Take 2 yards (2 m) of the orange warp thread and fold it in half. Pass one end behind the first warp on the left side. Then take the other end and pass it behind the second warp thread to the right. Then take the first end and pass it behind the third warp thread and continue along until you have twined all the way across. Tie an overhand knot to hold the twining stitch in place.

9

Snip off the loops at the end of the piece, leaving a little fringe. You can also tie knots in adjacent pairs of warp yarns for additional security.

10

Trim any tails from the back of the project.

soumak roving rainbows weaving

12 × 18-inch (30 × 46 cm) loom

cotton rug warp

bulky-weight yarn; I used We Are Knitters The Wool (100% wool; 87 yards [80 m] per 7-ounce [200 g] ball) in Natural

roving; I used a Mixed Merino Wool Bag from Paradise Fibers, in Beautiful Brights: 10 colors, 1 oz (25 g) each

variety of hand-dyed and hand-spun fibers; I used Roving Textiles

scissors

weaver's sword (optional)

yarn needle or shuttle

weaver's fork (optional)

12-inch (30 cm) dowel or rod for hanging

COLOR STORY

bright rainbow

TECHNIQUES

double-d locks, basic tabby, bubble, soumak, lark's head knots, rya knots

165

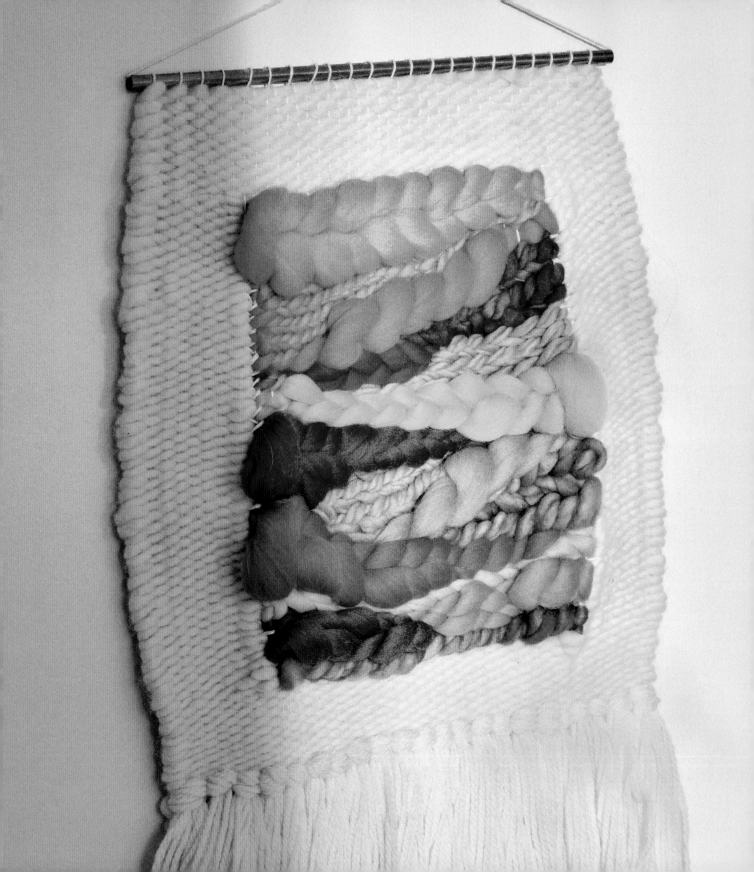

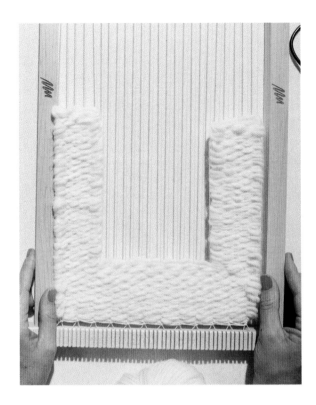

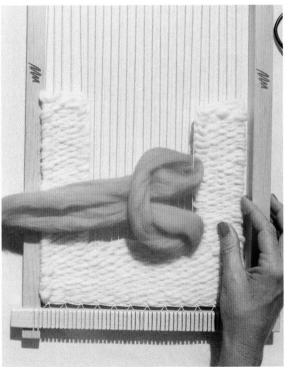

1

Warp up your loom. Tie your cotton rug warp on the top-left peg and then draw it down to the bottom left peg, around, and back up and around the second peg on the top left. Continue all the way along from left to right across your loom until you reach the last, top-right peg. You want to check your tension, and you may need to readjust. Weave in your weaver's sword if you want to weave faster.

2

Create a row of DOUBLE-D LOCKS (see page 28). Measure out a piece of warp thread 4 times the width of your warp. Fold it in half and wrap around the first 2 warps at the bottom end of your loom on the right side. This should be the loom end that does *not* have the knots tied to begin and end the warp. Hold the loop at the bottom of the warp and wrap the tails around and over the first 2 warps. You should see a capital D formed. Pass the tails through the middle of the D. This is your first D lock. Do this twice on the same pair of warps to create the lock; you have just tied a double half-hitch. Then move across to the next pair of warps and repeat. Continue all the way across your loom, from right to left. If you have any tails left, just weave a row or two of BASIC TABBY (see page 20) until the tails run out. Basic tabby goes over and under, over and under, all the way across. It doesn't really matter if you begin over or under.

3

Now you need to prepare your fibers. I chose natural cream-colored Merino wool in a pencil roving as a border for this piece. You will need one length of 8 yards (8 m)—if your roving is thin and you want to weave faster, simply double it. Either thread your needle or load your shuttle. Begin weaving basic tabby at the bottom left across to the right. Check that the knots that connect your warp to the loom are at the opposite end of the loom.

4

Be sure to BUBBLE each row (see page 20) to ensure you are getting even tension all the way up your weave. Bubbling stops you from pulling too tightly across a pass of tabby.

5

When you get to the end of your first row, turn back and weave your second row directly above, from right to left. This row or pass should be the opposite of the first row. Be sure to bubble. Check that your ends are touching the first and last warps without bagging or pulling in.

6

Continue weaving until the yarn runs out. I wove 10 rows. Weave in your ends by turning back in on the weave; weave the opposite to the row above or below and then vertically back into the color you were just weaving. This will tuck the tail into the weave without its being visible from the front.

7

You have just woven the first tabby section of your piece. We are weaving upside down, from the top of the piece up to the bottom. By doing it this way, we are left with a nice, neat top to the weaving, with the loops already created using the warp threads.

8

Now we will weave the two side borders. Again, take about 4 yards (4 m) of The Wool in Natural. This time weave a section that is about 8 warp threads across on the left-most side of the weave. Then you can measure out another 4 yards (4 m) of the same yarn and weave a section that is about 8 warps wide on the right side of the weave.

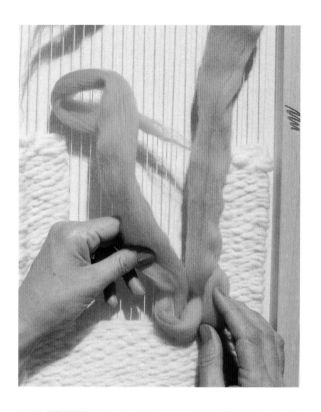

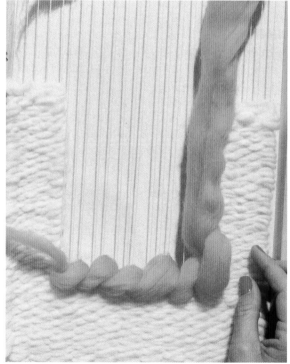

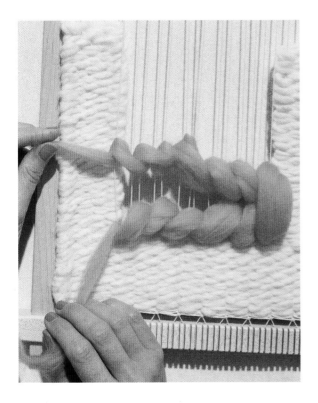
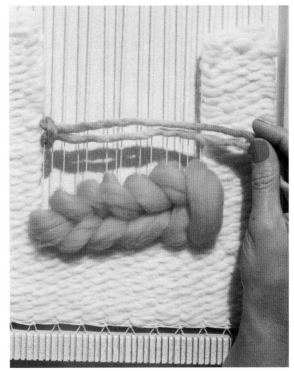

9

Now it is time to fill in the middle section with the rainbow SOUMAK stitch (see page 22). This is quite an organic process, and you will find that some fibers will fill up more space and some will behave in ways that you can't predict. My advice is to go with the flow. Soumak is a stitch that looks like a braid and is created by weaving two tails in different directions.

10

Prepare your fibers by creating a rainbow gradation with bright fibers of different weights and lengths. Then you will create a basic soumak with each fiber in order. I pulled the pieces of roving to the desired length and then pulled a bit of extra roving off the ends to create a tapered effect. This will give the braids a more varied look.

11

I used yellow roving for my first soumak stitch. Take about ½ yard (0.5 m) of roving and fold it in half. Pass the loop behind the right-hand warp and thread the 2 tails through the loop; this anchors the roving with a LARK'S HEAD KNOT (see page 27). Take one tail to create the first (bottom) row of soumak braid. Count 3 warps to the left and pass the tail behind and back from left to right. Be sure that the tail is pointing up. Count 3 warps to the left and pass the tail behind this warp from left to right. Continue along until you come to the end of the section. I created 8 soumak stitches.

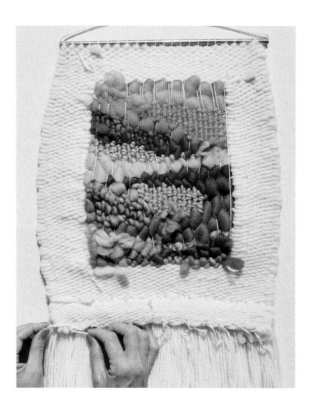

12

Now we will create the top half of the braid. Take the other tail and count 3 warps to the left. Pass the tail behind the warp from left to right. Be sure that the tail is pointing down. Then count 3 more warps to the left and pass the tail behind this warp from left to right. Continue along until you come to the end of the section. I created 8 soumak stitches. Tuck the ends away to the back in between the two layers of the braid.

13

To create a more varied, organic effect, choose a variety of thicknesses and shades of colors. You can build up a smaller area by creating soumak back and forth in descending numbers of warps. This can make an organic-looking triangle. You can mix it up by creating one row of soumak. When I choose a thinner fiber, I create a soumak stitch on every warp rather than counting 3 between each soumak stitch.

14

Fill in the rest of the void with rainbow soumak of various lengths.

15

Once the rainbow has been filled in, complete the white border using the cream pencil roving again, and tabby.

16

A line of white RYA KNOTS (see page 25) will create a smooth transition from the weave to the fringe. Measure out your yarn to your preference (my fringe was 12 inches/30 cm, so each length was 24 inches/60 cm) in The Wool in Natural and tie rya across the weave, tying knots on each pair of warp threads until you have completed the entire row. I like a fringe of about 1 foot on this weave, and so each length needs to be 2-feet as it hangs.

17

Finish off your weaving with 3 or 4 rows of tabby to secure your piece. This will sit under the fringe of rya knots, so you can use any yarn you have on hand. I like to finish my pieces with another row of double-D locks to really secure my weaving in place.

18

Then simply cut the bottom warps and tie some knots in the warp close to the bottom of the weaving, to hold the weaving where you want it to stay. Knotting adjacent pairs of warp ends works well.

19

Pop the loops off the top (remember where the top is; we wove this upside down) and pass a rod (or branch, or spoon—experiment!) through your loops until all the loops are on the rod. To hang the rod, tie a piece of yarn to each end. Lift up your weaving and admire your work!

beachy waves texture

18 × 20-inch (46 × 51 cm) loom

40 yards (37 m) cotton rug warp

a variety of bulky-weight yarn and roving, about 2–4 yards (2–3.5 m) of each; I used merino wool from We Are Knitters, Paradise Fibers, Roving Textiles, and Echoview Fiber Mill

cotton rope or cord for fringe

scissors

weaver's sword

yarn needle or shuttle

weaver's fork (optional)

20-inch (51 m) dowel or rod for hanging

COLOR STORY

nature inspired

TECHNIQUES

twining, basic tabby, bubble, soumak, knotting, rya knots

Note: The yarn colors shown in the Method differ from the finished project on page 173.

1

Warp up your loom. Tie your cotton rug warp on the top-left peg and then draw it down to the bottom-left peg, around, and back up and around the second peg on the top left. Continue all the way along from left to right across your loom until you reach the last, top-right peg. Wrap the warp thread around the last peg 2 times, but do not tie off yet. You want to check your tension, and you may need to readjust.

2

Check your warp tension. It should be springy and even all the way across and strum and vibrate when you pass your fingers across the warp threads. If the warp threads stick together, it is too loose. Correct the tension, and when you are happy with it, tie off on the top-right peg. Weave in your weaver's sword. And weave a barrier row of TWINING (see page 18).

3

Now you need to prepare your fibers and yarns. I chose a color gradation from light to dark, beginning with white and finishing with the darker blues and grays. You will need one length of 2 yards (2 m). Either thread your needle or load your shuttle. We want to create an undulating, wavy look. Weave a few full rows before beginning to shape your wave. Begin weaving BASIC TABBY (see page 20) at the bottom left, across to the right. Check that the knots securing the warp to the loom are at the opposite end. Basic tabby goes over and under, over and under, all the way across. It doesn't really matter if you begin over or under.

4

Be sure to BUBBLE (see page 20) each row to ensure you are getting even tension all the way up your weave.

5

When you get to the end of your first row, turn back and weave your second row directly above, from right to left. This row or pass should be the opposite of the first row. Be sure to bubble. Check that your ends are touching the first and last warps without bagging or pulling in.

6

Continue weaving until the yarn runs out. This wave shape will be quite organic. Begin your first row of the wave at the left-hand side of the loom, and weave only halfway across. Then turn back and tabby weave all the way back, but stop 2 or 3 warp threads before you get to the edge of the weave. On the next pass, you will need to stop 2 or 3 warps from the edge in both directions. These are organic shapes, so we want them to mimic nature. Nature is perfectly imperfect, so try to mix up the number of warps you leave at the edges so that your shape does not end

up looking like a triangle. If you run out of yarn, you can simply tie another length on and then make sure that this knot is angled to the back. Weave in your ends by turning back in on the weave into the color you were just weaving. This will tuck the tail into the weave without its being visible from the front.

7

Using the same fiber, create a smaller organic wave on the other half of the loom. This will give the illusion of a natural undulation. Beginning at the right side of the weave, weave in toward the center, but stop before you get all the way there. Turn back and weave a row, and stop and turn around before you get all the way back to the right side. Continue weaving back and forth, including progressively fewer warp threads for each row, until you have an organic curved shape. Weave in your ends.

8

Now we have a lovely undulating, curved shape to begin. Take the next fiber in your gradation color (mine is core-spun yarn from Echoview Fiber Mill in the color Hedwig). Weave a few rows of tabby all the way across. This is where you can really make a mess of your tension—keep an eye on your warp threads, and ensure they remain straight and separate. If they begin to pull in and touch, it will have an effect on your selvedges. I would suggest bubbling larger than you usually do, as your new weft needs to work evenly around the curves rather than simply straight across.

9

Now we will follow these lovely curves with SOUMAK stitch (see page 22). This is quite an organic process, and you will find that some fibers will fill up more space and some will behave in ways that you can't predict. My advice is to go with the flow. Soumak is a stitch that looks like a braid and is created by weaving 2 tails in different directions.

10

I chose roving for this section. Prepare your fibers. I pulled off pieces of roving to my desired length, about one arm's length, halved each piece lengthwise down the middle, and then pulled a bit of extra roving off the ends to create a tapered effect. This will give the braid a more varied look.

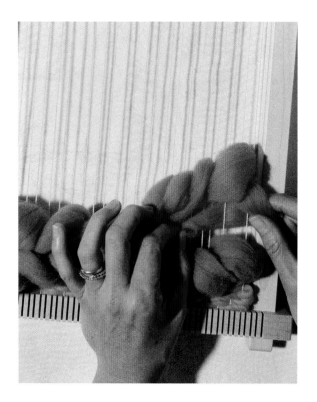

11

I used the Pearl color roving for my first soumak stitch. Tuck one end to the back of the weaving, about halfway to the middle. Take the other tail to create the first (bottom) row of soumak braid. Count 3 warps to the left and pass the tail behind and back, from left to right. Be sure that the tail is pointing up. Count 3 warps to the left and pass the tail behind this warp, from left to right. Continue along until you come to the end of the section. I created 6 soumak stitches.

12

Now we will create the top half of the braid. Take the other half of the roving and tuck the tail behind where the other stitch was created. Count 3 warps to the left. Pass the tail behind the warp from left to right. Be sure that the tail is pointing down. Then count 3 more warps to the left and pass the tail behind this warp from left to right. Continue along until you come to the end of the section. I created 8 soumak stitches. Tuck the ends away to the back in between the two layers of the braid.

13

It's time to incorporate some KNOTTED texture (see page 26) in the valley of the left-hand side of the weave. Prepare your yarns. Take 4 yards (4 m) of your yarn (I used We Are Knitters The Wool in Pearl) and run it back on itself 4 times, so you end up with 4 pieces of the same length, 1 yard (1 m). Tie overhand knots all the way along with random spacing. Use this yarn to weave basic tabby. Ensure these knots sit toward the front of the weave, to help create a random, organic texture.

14

You can create a different knotting look by knotting on the actual warp threads. When I do this technique, I like to leave the ends hanging toward the front to act as a small tassel. Begin by weaving across a couple of warp ends in tabby. When I come to a warp that I want to knot on, I simply turn the end of the weft back on itself with my right hand while holding a little loop of the slackened weft in my left. Twist the loop before passing the end through the loop, then continue passing along the row in the same tabby pattern. You will need to keep an eye on which warps need to be passed over and which need to be passed under. A weaver's sword can be very helpful at this point: Simply weave it through at the top of your piece and leave it turned up on edge to remind you which warps need to be passed under. After you have woven across a couple more warps, you can create another knot. These look best when created randomly.

15

To create a more varied, organic effect, choose a variety of thicknesses and shades of color. You can build up a smaller area by weaving back and forth in descending numbers of warps. You can do this with tabby, soumak, or knotting techniques, which can make organic-looking shapes. You can mix it up by creating one row of soumak, tabby, or knotting. When I choose a thinner fiber or yarn, I create a soumak stitch on every warp rather than counting 3 between each soumak stitch.

16

It is important to weave sections of basic tabby stitch to lock in areas with soumak, knotting, or other fancy stitches. The basic tabby will lock in and reset your warp. Once you are happy with your textural knotty and wavy piece, finish off the design by weaving sections of basic tabby to fill in the open areas, and then finish off with a few rows of tabby across the full width of the piece.

177

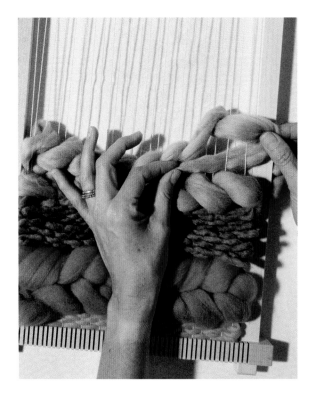

17

It's time to add your fringe. I chose to create each RYA KNOT (see page 25) with 3 lengths of cord measuring 1 yard (1 m) each. Start by taking one bunch of 3 lengths and folding them in half like the letter U. Lay this U across the first 2 warps on the left side of your weave. Pass the left side of the U ends under the first warp thread and back up between the first and second warps. Then pass the right side of the U ends under the second warp and back up between the first and second warps. Pull up the 6 ends and lay them flat across the top of your rya knot. You have completed your first rya knot. Continue tying knots on each pair of warp threads until you have completed the entire row.

18

Finish off your weaving with 3 or 4 rows of tabby to secure your piece. This will sit under the fringe of rya knots, so you can use any yarn you have on hand.

19

Then simply pull the warp loops off your loom and tie some knots in the warp close to the bottom of the weaving, to hold the weaving where you want it to stay. Remember that we wove this upside down, so that is the bottom we just finished.

20

One of the most satisfying parts of weaving is hanging your completed piece. Just as you did at the bottom of your weaving, you can pop the warp loops off their pegs at the top. As you go, pass a rod (or branch, or spoon—experiment!) through your loops until all the loops are on the rod. Be sure to pass the rod through opposite to the last row of tabby that you did. To hang the rod, tie a piece of yarn to each end. Lift up your weaving and admire your work!

continuous rya loop circle weaving

12 × 18-inch (30 × 46 cm) loom

30 yards (27 m) cotton rug warp

super-chunky yarn; I used Roving Textiles Superfluff: 20 yards (20 m) each in Dijon at Dawn and Cherry Melon, for the inside circle; 38 yards (35 m) in Sapphire Nights, for the background

44 yards (40 m) cotton string, for fringe; I used Mustard 5 mm from Mary Maker Studio

scissors

yarn needle or shuttle

12-inch (30 cm) dowel or rod for hanging

8-inch (20.5 cm) cardboard circle

fabric-marking pen or Sharpie

~~~

COLOR STORY

saturated jewel tones

TECHNIQUES

double-d locks, basic tabby, rya knots, knotted pile texture, dovetail

1

Warp up your loom. Tie your cotton rug warp on the top-left peg and then draw it down to the bottom-left peg, around, and back up and around the second peg on the top left. Continue all the way along from left to right across your loom until you reach the last, top-right peg. Wrap the warp thread around the last peg 2 times but do not tie off yet. You want to check your tension, and you may need to readjust. When you are happy with the tension, tie off on the top-right peg.

2

Create a barrier stitch of DOUBLE-D LOCKS (see page 28). These are essentially double half hitches that sit as a barrier between the rod and the weave. Then take 4 yards (4 m) of warp thread and fold it in half around the first 2 warp threads on the right side, closest to the rod. Leaving the loop at the bottom of the weave, lift the thread up and back to the left,

creating a capital D. Then loop under the pair of warps and through the inside of the D. Pull it tight and down toward the rod. Repeat on the first 2 warp threads. This creates two Ds, or a double D. Then move on to the second pair of warps and repeat. Carry on all the way along the warps and keep the DD knots close to the end of the loom. If you have any thread left over, simply weave a few rows of BASIC TABBY (see page 20) and weave the end back into itself.

3

Next you will need to grab a cardboard circle, 8 inches in diameter, or a dinner plate. Place it onto your weave where you want your design to be, then trace around it with a fabric marker. These often disappear when they get wet.

4

The best way to tackle a circle is to weave the tabby in sections around it. Begin with the first section between the rod and the circle.

5

Next weave sections 2 and 3. These will form the curves of the circle, from the top to the sides on both sides.

6

Now you should have half a circle of basic tabby weave, with a window of open half circle. We will begin to fill this in with RYA KNOTS (see page 25), creating a knotted pile texture. You will need to measure out about 4 yards (4 m) of yarn and ball it up or create a butterfly of yarn to keep it tidy.

7

Find the left side of the bottom of the circle. Pick up 2 warp threads and create a starter knot. Take the end of your ball of your second color of yarn and place it over the top of the 2 warps, with the tail pointing toward the left. Wind the tail under the first warp and through the middle of the 2 warps. Hold this in place while you pass the ball around the second warp and through the middle of the pair. Pull down to tighten the knot. This is very similar to the basic rya knots that we use to create fringe. Tuck the tail behind the weave.

8

Now we will create our first rya loop. Pick up the next 2 warp threads to the left. Take the ball of Mustard and pass it in front of the left-side warp and back under to the left. Pull it through until you leave a little loop the size you want. Take the ball and pull

it over the 2 warps from left to right, and then back under the second warp from right to left. It should pop up between the pair of second warps. Repeat across the first row of your circle, creating looped rya knots on each pair of warps and leaving a little loop between.

9

Now we need to lock in the loops with basic tabby weave. Weave 2 rows of tabby above the first row of continuous rya loops. This will keep our rya secure, as well as reset our warp and keep it neat. Be sure to include the last warp of the outer circle in the rows of tabby in a DOVETAIL (see page 30).

10

Our second row of rya loops will move from the right side of the circle to the left side. Pick up the first 2 warp threads to the right. Take the ball of yarn and

pass it in front of the right-side warp and back under to the right. Pull it through until you leave a little loop the size you want. Take the ball and pull it over the 2 warps from right to left, and then back under the second warp from left to right. It should pop up between the pair of second warps. Repeat across the second row of your circle, creating looped rya knots on each pair of warps and leaving a little loop between.

11

Weave 2 rows of tabby. Attach it to the sides of the circle using a dovetail.

12

Continue with 1 row of rya loops and 2 rows of tabby until you fill in the circle. I chose to change colors halfway up the circle to create a sunset/moonrise design.

183

13

Once the circle has been filled in, weave basic tabby around the outside, following the diagram in order of sections 5, 6, and finally 7 to complete the woven section of the weave.

14

Now we are going to add a layer of rya fringe. You will need to cut about 3 lengths of yarn for each rya. I am using colored cotton rope. The length of the fringe that you cut will determine the length of your fringe. I made my lengths by winding yarn around a book, so my lengths were approximately 24 inches (60 cm). When folded into a rya knot, they measured 12 inches (30 cm).

15

Take one bunch of 3 lengths and fold them in half like a smile or the letter U. Lay this U across your first two warps on the left-hand side of your weave. Pass the left side of the U ends under the first warp thread and back up between the first and second warps. Then pass the right side of the U ends under the second warp and back up between the first and second warps. Pull up the 6 ends and lay them flat across the top of your rya knot. You have completed your first rya knot.

16

Continue across the weave, tying knots on each pair of warp threads until you have completed the entire row. If it does not look full enough, you can create a second row of rya knots on alternate warps to fill in the gaps.

17

Finish your weaving off with 3 or 4 rows of tabby to secure your piece. I used the same cotton rope I used for the rya knots. I like to finish with another row of double-D locks to secure my weaving.

18

Then simply cut the warp threads from your loom and tie some knots in the warp close to the bottom of the weaving, to hold the weaving where you want it to stay. Remember that this end you just finished is the bottom, and these knots will be hidden by the rya fringe.

19

Pop the warp loops off their pegs at the top (remember that this is where the weaving started). As you go, pass a rod (or branch, or spoon—experiment!) through your loops until all the loops are on the rod. To hang the rod, tie a piece of yarn to each end. Lift up your weaving and admire your work!

split woven necklace

COLOR STORY

analogous neutral tones with gold accent

TECHNIQUES

rya knots, twining, basic tabby, double-D locks

12 × 18-inch (30 × 46 cm) loom

6 yards (6 m) of cotton rug warp

thin cotton cord in 4 shades, 11 yards (10 m) of each; I used Coloured Cotton Warp Cord by Mary Maker Studio in Mustard, Dusty Mustard, Amber, and Cinnamon

scissors

yarn needle or shuttle

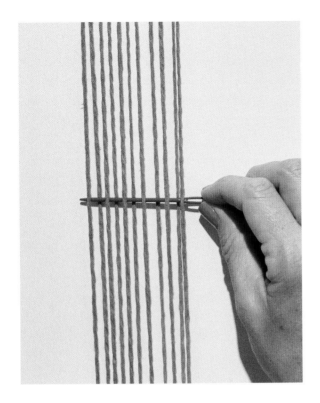

1

Warp up your loom using cotton rug warp. I chose to make my warp 18 warp ends across. Be sure to tie on and off at the top end, ensuring an even number of warp ends. I chose a fine warp sett on this project. This means that I want a close density: as many warp threads as possible in a small width. This can be achieved if you put 2 warp ends in the same slot when warping up.

2

Check your warp for even and correct tension. It should be springy and even all the way across, and should strum and vibrate when you pass your fingers across the warp threads. If the warp threads stick together, it is too loose. Correct the tension, and when you are happy with it, tie off the end at the top of the loom.

3

First we need to create the base of the necklace. This won't be seen but will hold our first layer of RYA KNOTS (see page 25). First work 2 rows of TWINING (see page 18) across the width of the necklace. Then thread your needle or load your shuttle with yarn. This is your weft. Begin weaving BASIC TABBY (see page 20) at the bottom left, and weave 8 rows.

4

Now we need to bring the shape to a point. We will do this by creating steps. The first step will come in two warps on either side. Weave 4 rows of tabby on the 14 central warp yarns. Then move to the next step: Come in 2 more warps from each side and weave 4 more rows of tabby on the central 10 warp ends. The top step will be just 6 warps across in the middle of the shape and 4 rows high. Cut your weft, and weave the tail back into the shape from top to bottom.

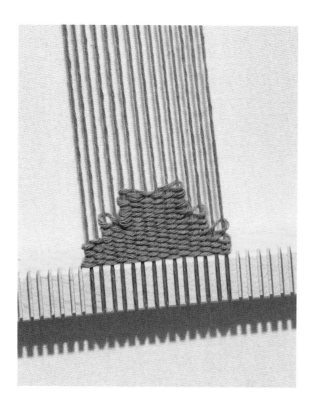

5

Cut some lengths of thin yarns to create your first row of rya knots. Mine are 20 pieces thick and 8 inches (20 cm) long (4 inches/10 cm once knotted into the work). Create a row of rya knots. You should have a pair of warps at each step to tie a rya knot on. The top row will have 6 warps on which to create 3 rya knots.

6

We need to lock the first row of rya knots in with a block of tabby, but first we need to fill in the sides. We will weave the reverse of the first block, weaving one side first and then the other. Start at the bottom of the steps on the left, and weave the left 2 warps for 4 rows. Then weave the left-most 4 warps for 4 rows. Then weave 6 warps for 4 rows. Then cut the weft and weave the tail back into the weave.

7

Repeat on the right side. Then continue to weave all the way across for 12 rows. This is the tabby that locks in our rya.

8

Repeat step 4 with the original color. This will create the next stepped block pattern.

9

It's time for a color change. Repeat steps 6 to 8 with a new color, only this time without the rya knots. Once you have woven 12 rows, split the weaving in two, exactly in the middle, and weave the left side for the steps, and then the right side. You will need to finish each block with the same steps that we created earlier.

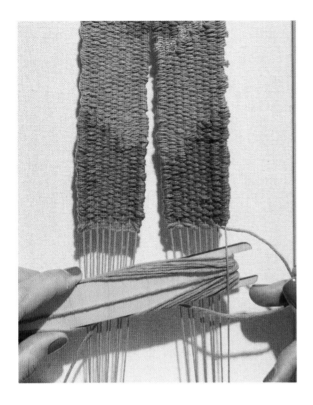
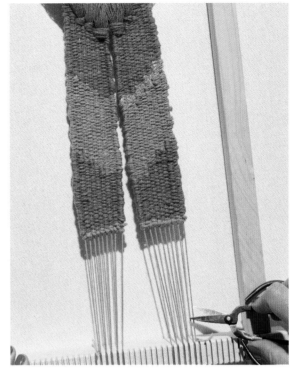

10
Add a second row of rya knots, but these will be slightly shorter.

11
Lock these in with the same block pattern and weave up the 2 separate lengths of the necklace, continuing the pattern.

12
Once you are happy with the length of the sides, it's time to lock it all in with DOUBLE-D LOCKS (see page 28). This is a great way to bind weaving or even create negative space. As this is a fine project, we will create the locks on every warp thread rather than in pairs. Take a piece of yarn and loop it around the right-most of the right-side warp. Push the loop down toward the weave and take the tails back over the warp to the left, creating a D, and back under the warp through the loop created by the D. Do this

twice, creating a second D lock (double-D lock). Then move across to the next warp on the left and repeat. Continue all the way across the right-hand section, then weave the tails back in.

13
Repeat on the left-hand side section of the necklace, starting on the right and ending on the left.

14
Slip the loops off the top of the loom and create 3 braids or twisted plied fringes on each side. Do this by taking an equal number of warp ends in both hands and firmly twisting each bundle separately to the left, and then placing them together and firmly twisting them back to the right. Secure the twist with an overhand knot. If you want to add bit more length, you can add an extra piece of thread between the braids and wrap it around the new piece over the ends of the braids. Weave the ends back into the wrapping.

189

resources

Here are some favorite sources for looms, fiber, and other supplies.

1AZColorworks
HAND-DYED MERINO WOOL
www.etsy.com/shop/1AZColorworks

Ashford Handicrafts
SPINNING/WEAVING EQUIPMENT AND FIBER
www.ashford.co.nz

Balfour & Co
WEAVING SUPPLIES
www.balfourand.co

Echoview Fiber Mill
www.echoviewnc.com

Funem Studio
WEAVING SUPPLIES
funemstudio.com

Great Ocean Road Woollen Mill
gorwm.com.au

Maryanne Moodie
WEAVING SUPPLIES
www.etsy.com/shop/MaryanneMoodie

Mary Maker Studio
WEAVING SUPPLIES
marymakerstudio.com.au

Niroma Studio
WEAVING SUPPLIES
niromastudio.com

Roving Textiles
LOOMS AND FIBER/YARN
www.rovingtextiles.com

We Are Knitters
YARN
www.weareknitters.com.au

Wool and the Gang
YARN
www.woolandthegang.com

acknowledgments

The journey of this, my second book, has been made possible by only the best people.

Thank you to my editor, Meredith Clark, for encouraging me (with a firm hand) throughout the process. I would love to acknowledge the endless work of managing editor Lisa Silverman and tech editor Nancy Reid for helping to wrangle my thoughts into line, and my designer, Laura Palese, for making this fun and accessible vision come to life. And everyone else in my Abrams family who came together to pin my dreams to the page.

It is always a complete pleasure working with my photographer, Lauren Bamford—a consummate professional and artistic visionary.

Thank you to my clients and customers over the years who have supported my work and helped me further along this woven road than I ever dreamed possible.

My extended and chosen family and friends, thank you for encouraging me to pursue this dream, even when it felt like a nightmare.

And to Aaron, Murray, and Rudi—for living these past ten years of dream weaving together and creating the rich tapestry of life. You have made it more beautiful and intricate than my hands alone could.

Editor: Meredith A. Clark
Designer: Laura Palese
Design Manager: Darilyn Lowe Carnes
Managing Editor: Lisa Silverman
Production Manager: Kathleen Gaffney

Library of Congress Control Number:
2021946853

ISBN: 978-1-4197-5302-2
eISBN: 978-1-64700-230-5

Printed and bound in the United States
10 9 8 7 6 5 4 3 2 1

Abrams books are available at special discounts
when purchased in quantity for premiums
and promotions as well as fundraising or
educational use. Special editions can also be
created to specification. For details, contact
specialsales@abramsbooks.com or the address
below.

Abrams® is a registered trademark of Harry N.
Abrams, Inc.

ABRAMS The Art of Books
195 Broadway, New York, NY 10007
abramsbooks.com